Trainwreck

MY LIFE

~~AS AN~~

~~IDIET~~

~~IDIOT~~

IDOIT

JEFF NICHOLS

A Touchstone Book

Published by Simon & Schuster

New York   London   Toronto   Sydney

Author's Note: Certain names and identifying characteristics have been changed. Certain incidents have been compressed and reordered. And (I hope) some comic license has been taken.

 Touchstone
A Division of Simon & Schuster, Inc.
1230 Avenue of the Americas
New York, NY 10020

A previous edition of this work was published as *The Little Yellow Bus* in 2007 by Outskirts Press.

First Touchstone trade paperback edition July 2009

TOUCHSTONE and colophon are registered trademarks of Simon & Schuster, Inc.

For information about special discounts for bulk purchases, please contact Simon & Schuster Special Sales at 1-800-456-6798 or business@simon andschuster.com.

Designed by Elliott Beard

Manufactured in the United States of America

10 9 8 7 6 5 4 3 2 1

Library of Congress Cataloging-in-Publication Data

Nichols, Jeff.
Trainwreck : my life as an idiot / Jeff Nichols.
    p. cm.
    "A Touchstone book."
    1. Nichols, Jeff. 2. People with disabilities—United States—Biography.
3. Learning disabilities—United States—Case studies. 4. Alcoholics—
United States—Biography. 5. Drug addicts—United States—Biography.
6. Comedians—United States—Biography. 7. Slackers—United States—
Biography. 8. WASPs (Persons)—Biography. 9. Substitute teachers—New
York (State)—New York—Biography. 10. New York (N.Y.)—Biography.
I. Title. II. Title: My life as an idiot.

CT275.N348A3 2009
362.196'858890092—dc22 [B]

                                                                    2009015454

ISBN 978-1-4165-9916-6
ISBN 978-1-4391-1286-1 (ebook)

To Mom and Dad

PROLOGUE

I spent years trying to get this memoir published. It is an understatement to say that this book was not originally embraced by the New York literary community. Hoping to be the toast of the town, I was basically told to go out and purchase a shredder.

I recall one literary agent suggesting that I give it an old-fashioned burial at sea. Another told a friend of mine that I should rename the book *My Life as an Idoit*. I loved that and immediately added it to the title.

At one point, trying to capitalize/exploit the learning-disabled "industry/marketplace," I tried to make it purely a self-help book for the learning disabled called *The Little Yellow Bus*. In many ways I still believe this book is useful for the LD person. Granted, I am not a doctor, lawyer, or CEO of a Fortune 500 company, and, as one friend sarcastically but astutely points out, in my life I have "overcome very little to accomplish nothing." While his opinion may have some merit, I disagree. I may have had a combined score of 480 on the SAT, but I did manage to pass the US Merchant Marine captain's exam, which was an accomplishment, considering that many people (over 50 percent) fail it the first time they take it. I have also been paid for close to one hundred articles in various publications, including *Penthouse*, *The Fisherman* magazine, and the *New York Post*. Also, despite my often guttural and slurred speech, I did manage to make a modest living as a stand-up comedian for twelve years and was an opening act for many top national draws.

The problem with the self-help book angle was that I basically wrote my horrific story and then just lifted a bunch of AA slogans and stuck them at the end, suggesting, for example, that learning-disabled people take "one day at a time" and that they "should give time time." My weak effort was obviously transparent. Since then, I believe I have given the story more thought and effort.

I went on to write it as I really saw it, as a lighthearted comedy, and some people have told me that the book is one of the funniest things they have read in a while. Others found it too episodic and disturbing. I battled so long with agents who often bit but did not commit, that I decided to publish it myself, if only for vanity's sake.

This memoir somehow, someway, made it into the hands of one of the top independent film companies in the country, This Is That Productions, which has made films such as *The Savages*, *Eternal Sunshine of the Spotless Mind*, *21 Grams*, and *Friends with Money*. Eventually a movie was made based on this book starring Seann William Scott (Stifler of the *American Pie* flicks),

Gretchen Mol (*The Notorious Bettie Page*), and Jeff Garlin (*Curb Your Enthusiasm*).

I enjoyed many aspects of the film. Some of the scenes were powerful and insightful. Difficult subjects and themes like parental enabling (a subject that I took lightly, if not mocked, in this book) were illuminated and seriously explored in the film. I say bravo to that. I think the director and screenwriter, Tod Williams, did a fine job interpreting my work. He is a talented man and did more or less what he wanted to do. (I can only imagine how difficult it is to make a movie.) The fact of the matter is that festival audiences from Seattle to Michigan to New York liked the movie as did *Variety* magazine.

But I do believe that some of the, if I may, flat-out balls-to-the-wall humor and spirit in which I wrote the memoir simply did not make it into the film. So here it is. Thank you for reading it, and let me know what you think. Jeffnichols65@yahoo .com.

SO THE KID HAS
SOME PROBLEMS

Growing up, I had severe learning disabilities like dyslexia and attention deficit disorder way before they were buzzwords. I could not read or write until the seventh grade. I had a speech impediment and what was mentioned as possibly a mild case of Tourette's syndrome. Mention Tourette's and everybody has an image of a madman screaming "cunt motherfucker!" in a crowded movie theater. As with all learning disabilities, there is no one conclusive test that confirms Tourette's. A diagnosis of various symptoms is made over time. On one of my many doctor trips over the years one of them noticed a conspicuous shoulder tic that I had had for about a year and linked that with some involuntary hand clapping and head scratching I experienced from time to time. He wanted to know if I had ever been diagnosed with Tourette's. Of course, I was horrified at the suggestion. At the time there was no formal diagnosis, but he suggested we watch the symptoms closely. Since then there still has been no formal diagnosis of Tourette's. More on this later.

In any case, I couldn't manage to break free from the confines of special education until somehow, with help from CliffsNotes, I made it through the respected Hobart College in upstate New York. I graduated with a BA in English as well as a serious addiction to drugs and alcohol. The amount of drugs and alcohol consumed by students at Hobart in the mid-'80s was massive and is probably worthy of a study of its own. Really. My own intake of cheap keg beer coupled with dangerous drugs left me virtually unemployable (classic burnout).

I come from what many would consider a privileged background. My mother's family was once a large landowner in England, and at one point my grandfather's wool company was one of the largest on the East Coast. But "privileged" is probably not the right word; my grandfather was certainly a wealthy man and were not starving by any means, but my sister and I did not have a lot of perks, considering our Park Avenue address. My sister, Jenny, used to profess that she was the "poorest kid at Kent" (a prestigious prep school in Connecticut). After all, for some time we were primarily living off my father's modest income as a magazine editor and writer, but then, rent on Park Avenue for a three-bedroom apartment was only $500. One must remember that it was the 1970s and people were not exactly clamoring to live in Manhattan as they do now. In fact, I believe it was the opposite. While it was a cultural center and the financial capital of the world, the crime rate was simply too high to attract people who wanted to raise families.

Everyone has seen the pictures of New York City in the 1970s.

Central Park was a giant dust bowl with a half-empty reservoir in the middle of it. There were no well-groomed trails or well-maintained gardens. No one would ever have considered venturing into the park after dusk or alone, the way they do now.

Drugs were pedaled everywhere in the seventies; no one would consider living on the Upper West Side or Lower East Side—Seventy-second Street and Broadway was dubbed "Heroin Circle." The most defining thing I remember about living in Manhattan back then was that people got mugged . . . a lot! I mean all the time. My step-grandmother, a first generation immigrant from Ireland, living in an Irish holdout in the Bronx, was mugged three times (once violently) for her bingo money. (She could not tell you who the vice president was, but could work five boards no problem.) I was held up at least five times. Small stuff mostly, a skateboard (with new Red Road Runner wheels and trucks), twenty bucks, my watch. Packs of urban youth would walk up and down the subway cars and torment whomever they wanted to. No one would ever consider riding on the last two cars of a subway train. We all sat in the middle cars huddled for safety. Purse-snatching was not something you would see in movies, but rather witness with your own eyes—some guy running down a crowded sidewalk with someone's bag and the victim yelling, "Stop that guy!"

Park Avenue and Fifth Avenue were always opulent, well-kept boulevards, but Third Avenue at Eighty-sixth Street was considered seedy and off limits to me and my sister. I don't like it when I hear people romanticize the past: "You know, Times Square used to have a great seedy element to it." While this may be the case (I visited the peep shows from time to time stoned with my high school friends), generally crime has receded into the background. What Giuliani, coupled with a strong economy, did for the city is amazing. A safer place is a better place.

Anyway, enough of that. The point is I have managed to blast through a substantial (100G) trust fund and, at thirty-five, I am a trainwreck of a man. I have no steady job, no permanent home. I have performed stand-up comedy and worked as a New York City substitute teacher. Two years ago I was arrested on Long Island, New York, for selling fish out of the trunk of my 1985 Dodge Diplomat. Now, if I could have looked into a crystal ball upon graduating from college at twenty-one and saw myself with no wife or children, renting a room at the Y, and selling porgies (fish), I would have probably taken a gun to my head. But, lucky for me, becoming a thirty-five-year-old loser is like diabetes—a gradual, progressive thing. One bad job dovetails with another, and suddenly selling fish out of the back of your car becomes the next right thing. In fact, the first time I made a hundred bucks illegally selling fish I remember thinking, *Wow, I am doing pretty good!* Pretty good? For a sixteen-year-old, perhaps. The guys I graduated from college with run hedge funds on Wall Street. Well, I guess everything is relative. I remember that the rock band Talking Heads has a song called "Once in a Lifetime." One of the lyrics goes like this: "And you may find yourself in a beautiful house, with a beautiful wife. And you may ask yourself, well, how did I get here?" If I was forced to write a rendition of this song it would be more like: "You may wake up and ask yourself: What is this rash on my stomach and why do I work at Pathmark?"

I am one bad career decision away from living in a cardboard box or moving in with my father—the ultimate humiliation.

So, as of only a couple of years ago, my most efficient way

of getting cash was by bumming off my family. I have gotten so proficient at this that I could probably teach a class at the graduate level. Luckily, I do not live with Mommy anymore. For years I lived out in Queens, but the umbilical cord still went out of her apartment, traveled across the East Side and over the East River, right into my apartment. Even today a team of therapists armed with saws and axes are trying to sever it. I guess, when it comes down to it, I would rather have dealt with the subtle low self-esteem associated with borrowing money from my family than the tangible pain of working nine to five.

I am not sure what Dr. Phil would say, but parents with children who are afflicted with real learning disabilities (when I say "real" I am not talking about "slow"; I mean, I could not read or write at all) feel guilty and have a tendency to overcompensate and enable us. They may clean up your room for you, or not get appropriately mad at you, or impose inadequate punishment when you screw up. In my case my mommy would give me money. But all of that changed five years ago when some awful, awful person came along and screwed up all the fun, feeding my mommy with a bunch of propaganda that she was "enabling me" blah blah. One day, when I stopped by her apartment and asked her for some loot, to my amazement and horror, she told me no. And that, get this, every time she gave me money she was "cutting my balls off." Imagine hearing this from your mother. That she is cutting your balls off!

Keep in mind, I was good at what I did—really, really good. She stunned me, no doubt about it. No one wants to hear his mother say "I am cutting your balls off," no matter how accurate it might be. I was staggered. But I collected myself and used what I thought was a brilliant analogy. "Look, Mommy, you make a good point, but theorize with me a second: if you take a bear that has been in captivity for his whole life, nurtured and fed by humans, then throw it out in the wild, do you think that bear will survive?" That line got me probably another two hundred bucks, but after that I was cut off.

First off, I must admit that I am writing this opus with a certain degree of desperation. Back in college I found it necessary, while others were studying, to snort something like a kilo's worth of the hideous designer drug ecstasy up my enormous nose, wiping out millions of productive and healthy dancing brain cells in the process. I fear that eventually my last two neurons will betray me, saying something along the lines of, "Look, somehow you managed to get rid of all our friends and fellow workers that helped us to process information and remember names. You have been pushing us to the limit, sustaining us with only wretched black coffee and the occasional blast of nicotine, so we are out of here!" Then, like an old lawn mower that has been pushed too far without oil, there will be a big bang, some black smoke, and then a possibly pleasant but ultimately unproductive state of dementia. I could go on at length about the long-term horrors of ecstasy abuse (chronic paranoia, bone marrow loss), but let me cut to the crudest, most effective deterrent that I tell college kids when I perform: "I did a lot of ecstasy twenty years ago, and today my dick only gets hard in the middle!" . . . So don't do it!

So, while I have this brief window of clarity, please indulge me in my story. At this point you're thinking: *Why do I want to read an autobiography written by a nobody?* To this, I say "Good point." You may also be thinking: *Here's another writer shamelessly exploiting his life—and handicaps—for a book.* Again, I commend you for your astute grasp of reality. In an effort to establish complete candor, I will take it a step further and confess that my primary motivation for writing, or performing stand-up comedy for that matter, is to date hot women (which certainly has not worked so far). There are many success stories of people—high-profile politicians and professional athletes—who have overcome severe learning disabilities to ultimately reach monumental success. Be warned. This is not one of those stories.

THE PERFECT STORM

In *The Perfect Storm,* by Sebastian Junger, three different weather patterns conspire to create the ultimate storm. My "storm" has three ingredients: vicious learning disabilities (in my years as a stand-up comic I used to joke that my SATs were so low that my entire school district lost funding), an insatiable appetite for drugs and alcohol, and the fact that I am a WASP.

At one point in history, the WASPs—aggressive imperialists that they were—conquered and then ruled the free world. Now it seems that we are a dying breed. Perhaps it is some sort of cosmic payback. Most WASPs, and I know there are some exceptions, have a tendency to sit around and wait to inherit money and various neurological diseases. Hopefully, in that order. (There were a lot of inbred folk on the *Mayflower,* don't you know. Put in the crudest terms—we all fucked each other back on that island. You can't find a more WASPy name than Parkinson's.) You show me a couple of pale-skin twins with Coke-bottle glasses and I bet they can be traced back to England. Obviously I am generalizing, but a lot of WASPs seem to be in a perpetual "holding pattern." When was the last time you saw a WASP help out another WASP? Sure, we will get together at the Union Club for a game of squash and a drink, but I will submit that we lack the solidarity of, say, the Irish, Koreans, or Jews. What I am saying is, I can't help my poor work ethic and weak libido (we simply can't fuck well—but we are great bankers); I was saddled with these apathetic, privileged genes at birth.

DYSLEXIA

Let's talk now about my specific learning disabilities. I have been diagnosed with dyslexia and attention deficit disorder (ADD). Dyslexia, I believe (some don't), is a real and powerful biological and neurological phenomenon. A severe case of dyslexia can render a person unemployable and put tremendous stress on the individual and his or her family. This condition does not discriminate; it can affect anyone regardless of his or her intelligence level.

A friend of mine, Max, with whom I graduated from high school, simply could not read at all. Max also had horrible spelling and handwriting. Today, Max is a prolific artist whose works sell for up to a hundred grand a piece. His art has been shown in many museums and galleries across the world.

Another friend, Jim, was performing so poorly in middle school that he was sent to a BOCES program. (The New York State Board of Cooperative Educational Services provides special programs and resources for kids who learn differently.)

That meant that Jim was so difficult that his case was actually contracted out—that, folks, is a severe case of dyslexia. Jim, however, made lemonade out of lemons, and, after a brief stint of dealing drugs and a couple of stays at reform schools, he used his strong interpersonal skills to learn about the contracting business. Ten years later, he started his own construction company in Florida and is married with two great kids.

Finally, another friend, Mark, was told by a guidance counselor that he should not bother applying to college. Instead, his parents hired a good tutor, and while he still struggled with English, he developed a strong aptitude for math. I was lucky enough to be standing next to Mark when we got the results of his SAT. Though his verbal was rock bottom, a 220, his math score, a 780, was in the top percentile in the country. Mark went to college on a few scholarships.

Aside from chronic sloppiness and the obvious mixing up of words and letters, another common denominator with LD people is that we are all (with the exception of Mark's 780 in math) horrific standardized test takers—absolutely awful. What the dyslexics do to the national curve is downright contemptible. Even worse than test taking is our inability to read aloud publicly; it is actually comical. By ourselves we can usually labor through a book with some comprehension, but when we have to perform in front of a group, like a collective root canal, it is an agonizing experience for everyone involved. Show me a man who breaks out in a rash when he is asked to read aloud, and I will show you a dyslexic person. Is it any wonder that most learning-disabled people, in an effort to take the edge off and eliminate embarrassment, crawl into a vodka bottle any chance they get?

DYSLEXIA AND THE WORKPLACE

"We dyslexics are discriminated against!" my old friend Tim used to profess. Tim was referring to our plight in the workplace. To be fair, I should add that Tim had a daily pot habit. However, his point is not without some merit.

Unfortunately, capitalism rarely slows its wheels to accommodate the learning disabled. There simply is not enough time. If you happen to be saddled with a severe learning disability and find yourself gearing up for the workforce, get ready to hear two words a lot: "You're fired." Sometimes, these words will be cloaked in more euphemistic terminology like "We are downsizing," or "I don't think this is going to work out," or "Look, this job is not for everyone." When the economy is good, the learning disabled can usually find something (our slowness has to be tolerated because the workplace needs bodies), but I have found that when the economy is bad the learning disabled, on a superficial level reeking of incompetence, are the first to get their walking papers. After years of working on fishing boats in Montauk, New York, I realize that I am not a proactive employee, rather I am reactive. This could be distilled to this formula: They yell, I do.

Half the time we dyslexics don't even get job interviews because our handwriting is so illegible. Dysgraphia coupled with our awful phonetic spelling means our applications are never even considered. Learning-disabled people often never get through the initial screening process. This makes sense, as most employers are inundated with applications and are looking to lighten their loads. Eliminating any applications with pigeon scratch will help them thin down their pile.

In defense of dyslexics, let's face it—when it comes to spelling, the English language sucks. The rules suck, as do the exceptions to the rules. "And sometimes *y*?" What does that mean? Could this be a little more vague? Is it *-ible* or *-able*, *threw* or *through*? Do I *preform* or *perform*? I don't know! I would submit that the spelling rules are a form of tyranny for the dyslexic. I was not necessarily a dumb kid, but in high school I would misspell just about every word. A dictionary is of little use to the phonetic speller. Even spell check on a computer, while helpful at times, is not sympathetic or accommodating to the phonetic speller. It can betray us. For whatever reason, I never include *r* when I write the word *first*. Spell check on a computer, as good as it is, does not know that I want *first*, so it sees *fist* and leaves it alone.

It seems as though the people who wrote the English language purposely tried to mess us up. Here is a tangible example: *f* and *ph*. Pardon my Phrench but what the phuck is up with this? A comic friend named Jackie called and left a message on my answering machine to tell me about a big thousand-dollar comedy gig that she could not do and I could have. I had, of course, lost Jackie's number, but I knew her address and called information to get the number. I spelled her last name like it sounds—"Fallen." Who the hell would not? The operator informed me that there was no such listing. I tried a few more times with various spellings but finally gave up, figuring that, like a lot comics I know, Jackie had fled the country a step ahead of the law. Two years later I bumped into Jackie. When I told her that I was trying to get in touch with her, she informed me that her name is spelled with a *Ph*—Phelan. *Ph* cost me a thousand dollars. Can't this be amended somehow? I am just a guy trying to stagger through (threw) my miserable life. How about this new rule? If it sounds like *f*, let's use—oh, I don't know—the letter *f*! As unfair and arbitrary as the *ph* rule is, the English language does have some wonderful, phonetically friendly words: *Madagascar* and *mascara* come to mind.

Spelling traumas aside, there are some tasks that I am good at. I like jobs where I move things. When I get involved in a project that involves moving objects about, I can become quite diligent and effective. I guess some latent puritanical work ethic kicks in. As if trying to make up for every job I have ever messed up in the past, I work methodically.

For example, take moving a pile of wood: I have no problem moving one pile of wood to another pile. I could not pile it neatly, but nevertheless the wood would (that sounds funny) get moved.

A job that entails moving those big plastic colored balls, like the ones found in big bins at your local toy store, is perfect for me. I can get up in the morning, struggle through my cluttered, dysfunctional world of unopened bills, dirty dishes, and disillusioned friends, and somehow make it to work. Nirvana! The boss simply has to point to three big bins in a huge empty room. One of the bins, marked "A," has a bunch of red, white, and blue balls in it. The boss simply tells me to put all the red balls in one bin, put the blue balls (no pun intended) in another, and leave the white ones in the original bin. That's it.

There are no rules, regulations, guidelines, or middle-management intervention. I do not have to interact with anyone, and I can use whatever method I deem appropriate to move the balls. For instance, I can carry two and kick one along. I can even throw or juggle the balls. I can complete the task any way I damn well please so long as I meet my quota for the day.

Imagine the sense of accomplishment! I can meet my friends at a bar afterward, and when they ask me how my day was, I can answer, "Great. I moved all the blue and red balls! Go by and take a look!"

Then I will get good and liquored up. After all, I deserve a reward.

I know I am basically a spectator of life. I don't even have a credit card. I don't know how the fuck you human beings do it! Life is such a pain in the ass: the bills! the paperwork! the cleaning! the expired warranties!—everything breaks! And what about the kids! Humans have to be like ants in a nest always working, always moving. I am in awe of the mundane.

My own dysfunction is the reason I am extremely attracted to highly functional people. I remain baffled and amazed by people who invent things. It does not have to be a huge invention like the internet, GPS, or Viagra to impress me either. Like the other day, I was helping a friend move into a new apartment— that is a law: if you are a loser you must always be on call to help people move—and the boxes we put down to hold the door open kept sliding and proved generally ineffective. Some lady who lived in the building, noting our predicament, quickly sized up the situation and took a small piece of cardboard, folded it, and stuck it in the corner of the door, which held the door open firmly so we could lug our stuff in. A miracle! We looked at her in awe, as if she had just shot lightning out of her ass.

I have always been impressed also by the resourcefulness of the characters in books like *Lord of the Flies* or *Robinson Crusoe*. If I were stuck on a deserted island with the guys I hung out with in high school, there would be no irrigation systems, no pulleys, no rafts, and fire would be out of the question. When archaeologists would find our remains decades later, all they would find would be skeletons and a bunch of coconuts with holes in them. That is right—we would have been a colony of coconut fuckers.

TOURETTE'S SYNDROME

Tourette's syndrome is really nothing more than a severe case of hyperimpulsiveness, or, better put, the inability to control impulses. Not all people with Tourette's syndrome actually yell out. I believe too much caffeine will trigger this in me. I do not yell or talk out loud—yet. I feel that it is not a case of *if* but *when*. In fact, I came close to yelling out on a crowded subway the other day, professing "Good God! I'm lonely!" But, you see, I'm not sure I am afflicted with Tourette's. Rather, my impulse originated from the God-sized hole in my soul. The only symptom of Tourette's I have manifested so far is a slight motor twitch that becomes more pronounced when I am stressed.

And occasionally I rock back and forth and clap loudly. I know, very odd indeed. As one might imagine, this activity is usually interpreted as extremely antisocial and the clapping has even managed to get me evicted once. I must also add that when I am excited I tend to scratch my head, an action that certainly alarms and alienates people.

CHRONIC SLOPPINESS

I am a slob. (Doctors call it executive function deficit.) In some rural areas of Texas we are referred to as "pigs" or "cluster-fucks," not to be confused with "pack rats," which are separate entities altogether. My roommates in college used to refer to me, without affection, as "the Varmint."

Certainly I believe that my sloppiness has something to do with laziness, but also I believe it is related to my learning dis-abilities, and that somewhere in my brain is an organic chemical malfunction that relates to order. My sloppiness transcends the usual sloppiness of others. I am a Chronic Slob. I have several Chronic Slob theories that I believe are supported by anecdotal evidence from my own life.

The difference between a sloppy person and a Chronic Slob is that the Chronic Slob's mess cannot be re-created. Chronic sloppiness can be seen as a work of art. A team of scientists cannot replicate in ten hours what I can do to a hotel room in five minutes. A sloppy person has a three-day-old pizza box on his living room table. I have the same pizza box, but I do not have a living room table, or a living room for that matter. Inside the pizza box there is a W-2 form and a sock. A sloppy person will have three-week-old sheets on his bed.

I don't need a vacuum cleaner for my room; I need a back-hoe, although this matters not because I, the Chronic Slob, never clean. I simply move out, usually with all my worldly possessions, or those I can find, stuffed into two large green garbage bags. Once I was getting out of a cab in front of the apartment of a friend who was nice enough (or codependent enough) to let me move in with her. I put my two garbage bags on the curb and went to pay the cab driver. When I turned around, three people, not necessarily homeless, were riffling through my stuff. I had to fight them off. "Hey, that's my stuff," I protested. One of the guys claimed that he got there first. If it was not for the doorman, who knew me, a scuffle may have taken place.

Probably the most distinguishing characteristic between a Chronic Slob and a sloppy person is that the sloppy person does not like to be sloppy and is embarrassed by his slothfulness while the Chronic Slob prefers a good mess on some level. In fact, the Chronic Slob prefers chaos to order. He wallows in it. I know I should do things 1, 2, 3, but I prefer, or *must*, do things 1, 3, 2.

Chronic sloppiness transcends all economic and social boundaries. I passed a homeless person on the street the other day and found myself genuinely envious of the way he had structured his shopping cart. Here was order: his cans were organized; his newspapers were neatly tied up; and his tarp was folded perfectly. Quite impressive.

Chronic sloppiness, which has certainly tempered, if not ruined, any chance of a career or social success for me, is a common denominator among learning-disabled people. When it comes down to it, life is basically all about details and paperwork: bills, forms, applications, and occasional warrants. A healthy person with a clear mind takes the process in stride, deriving a sense of well-being when the task is done. A person with a learning disability sees day-to-day paperwork as a virtual meteor shower and becomes paralyzed. Sometimes, I will get my act together and pay some bills and enjoy that wonderful solace that comes when one "has his house in order." It all comes crashing down a month later when I am broadsided by the next set of bills, to my shock and outrage. "What is this phone bill? I just paid one of these last month!"

Countless times I have ventured into my room with the best intentions to clean. Armed with a broom and a bottle of Windex, I enter my den. The problem is that I have an inability to finish a task once I start it. I start sweeping. Move to the windows. The phone rings. Instantly, I am overwhelmed. Two minutes later I find myself in the corner, assuming the fetal position, frantically masturbating.

Sloppy people tend to smell bad but are embarrassed when it is brought to their attention. A Chronic Slob smells, but embraces it. I tend to enjoy my own musk and giggle when people point out with indignation that I reek.

I used to jest in my comedy act that the "worst day of the week for a slob is laundry day, because you spend half the morning rifling through scattered clothing on the floor trying to find something that you have not cum on." I also used to say that if "I had a vagina it would stink." (The first joke used to work well, apparently people identified with it; the second would elicit groans.)

When it comes to relationships I, the Chronic Slob, have problems. Many Chronic Slobs are charismatic; after all, they have to have some charm just to get through life. However, I would say that they are usually incapable of staying in a relationship.

I know women often look at me and think: *Project! Clean him up a bit! Get those gross teeth sandblasted! Get him to clip his nails! Buy some toilet paper for him!* Indeed, after all that work there might be a good product. However, the first time these optimistic women discover that I have dashed out a cigarette in their $100 container of moisturizer, they flee from me like a gazelle from a lion. A lot of guys are looking for a woman who wants to settle down; I am looking for someone who simply wants to settle.

Finally, if you want to have some fun, ask a Chronic Slob to empty his pockets. Sure, you will find the typical stuff, like candy wrappers and useless month-old receipts, but mixed in with the junk will be unexplainable stuff, like nine yards of snarled twine.

Stimulants, like the ridiculously overprescribed drug Ritalin, can help a Chronic Slob. They are delicious tasty little nuggets of productivity. Ritalin comes in delightful yellow five- and ten-milligram tablets. Wonderful (and festive) green and white twenty-milligram time-release capsules are also yummy. Take one pill and what was once a messy room becomes a highly functional factory.

The problem for me with Ritalin is that while I get what I paid for—the ability to focus—the drug does not have a "stop focus" gauge. What was once a casual glance at a girl's ass becomes an awkward glare. I have taken the drug and realized it was too much for me after polishing off the entire bottle in two days. (Is it bad to snort it?) I spent the entire time barricaded in my room organizing my underwear and sock drawer.

I do know that if Oscar from *The Odd Couple* were on Ritalin, he would be cleaner and neater, but he also might not be Oscar. Oscar would be focused, but focused primarily on getting his mitts on some more Ritalin. The goddamn stuff is addicting as hell.

WAS IT
THE POND WATER?

I can't recall the exact time I was relegated to special ed. My mother tells me it was when I was tested for the third grade. Ironically, I knew how to draw a circular shape and could name most of the states. But when asked the sum of two plus two or told to draw a square, I panicked. When asked to do the latter, I impulsively scribbled randomly on the page. I needed special attention because, quite simply, I was slow—slow in sports, slow in math, and especially slow in reading. When it came to the point that I read too slowly for the slowest reading group, the Trinity School in Manhattan called my mother in and said something like "Look, Mrs. Nichols, you have to get your kid out of our school. He's messing up the curve!"

I was a concern if not an embarrassment to my upper-class family. However, there was no lack of educators willing to put a positive spin on my predicament. Instead of calling me "dumb ass," they called me dyslexic.

Before I knew it, I was in a different private school, which we'll call "Martinson." I was in the smallest class imaginable. (A roll call of six kids, half of whom never showed up.) I'm not sure, but I think there might have been more teachers in the class than students. I also recall some mothers being present in the room. Back then, any student with a disability was lumped into one class. My brethren and I were all thrown together in one room that turned into a virtual smorgasbord of different disorders: muscular dystrophy, brain damage, ADD, ADHD, Tourette's, borderline autism, full-blown autism, hyperactivity, speech impediments, and, of course, dyslexia. I like to think that I was a jack-of-all-trades, blessed with a sprinkling of everything and definitely master of none.

The dynamics of my special ed classroom were fascinating. Of course, the hyperactive kids were the worst. Any teacher will confirm that one bad kid can ruin the whole day, and the average special ed class has at least three demonic warlords in it. What's more, these were the pre-Ritalin years. No Ritalin meant that kids with behavior problems were not anesthetized at all. Translation: these kids were absolute monsters and often had to be physically restrained. I can only imagine how disturbing and annoying this must have been to the smart, well-behaved physically disabled kids who were forced to share the same room.

In special ed the phenomena accumulate. During the first few weeks, students are confused and wonder why they are in such a small class with a such a mixed bag of afflictions. The kids who were physically fine but had behavior problems are wondering why they have to share a class with kids in wheelchairs. The kids in wheelchairs who are mentally fine, often brilliant (see Stephen Hawking), are wondering why they have to spend endless hours with kids who must have something the consistency of oatmeal between their ears. But, as the year progresses, familiarity often breeds solidarity, and alliances are formed. The special ed class becomes its own working entity: brains complement brawn and vice versa.

Out of this mess emerges a certain team unity. I'll cite an example from fifth grade. One day, my classmates and I decided to play rough while waiting for the elevator (a special ed perk). Joe (behavioral problem) pushed Jim (who was eventually expelled for repeatedly instructing teachers to "shave their asses"—behavioral problem), who in turn knocked over a student named Timmy (physically disabled).

Timmy was one of the most popular kids in the class. He used a walker, dragging his legs behind him. He had a great attitude and everybody loved him. Thus, everybody was aghast to see Timmy, who was always in the mix despite his precarious balance, sail straight backward and land on his head. We gathered around peering down at Timmy, who appeared to be unconscious. Somebody called the paramedics. We thought that was the end of Timmy.

I would like to say we missed him but, like all fifth graders, we had the attention spans of moths. However, before the day was up, the classroom door opened and everyone shrieked in delight at the sight of Timmy, beaming with pride and priceless happiness, apparently uninjured, or at least unchanged by the accident. It was tough to tell if there was damage. Timmy merely pulled himself toward his seat to rejoin our club.

At Martinson I became formally acquainted with the "little yellow bus." For a field day the whole school traveled to a park outside of the city. Buses pulled up in front of the school in the morning to transport the kids to the park. There were three traditional huge school buses, and behind them was a very conspicuous (at least to the kids who had to board it) little yellow bus complete with lifts and extra safety bars. Obviously this was for physically disabled kids, but those with no such afflictions were put aboard as well. We were further outraged to find that we would travel to a different park that was specifically designed for physically disabled kids. Once again my class was separated from the regular ed kids. Ironically, one of us, Jim, was one of the fastest kids in the school, but he was unable to compete against the regular ed kids because of this segregation.

THE DIAGNOSIS ACCORDING TO MY MOTHER, GOD BLESS HER

Though I was not a major behavioral problem at Martinson, I was no angel at home. My mother did not help matters, God bless her. She spoiled me rotten. An optimistic Christian Scientist, she woke me up every morning by coming into my room and professing, "This is the day the Lord has made, let us rejoice and be glad in it!" To which I would screech, "Get the fuck out of my room!" I am told this was around the time when I started to involuntarily clap and rock back and forth like a dog being sent unceremoniously off to obedience school.

My poor mother was forced to send me off to boarding school at a remarkably young age—when I was around twelve, after she and my father had divorced—where I could get some desperately needed special attention, not unlike an unruly cocker spaniel. However, that was not going to be so easy. As early as grammar school, I was already using chemicals to alter my mood (express lane to Junkieville), mostly through stuffing my face. Once, after getting cut from the junior varsity soccer team, I stole a large box of Good Humor toasted almond ice cream bars (delicious, by the way), from a local A&P supermarket. I parked my butt on a stoop, and ate every last one of them. I do not believe that stealing and overeating are consistent with the profile of a healthy child.

In addition to being overweight, I was an unmitigated klutz. Looking back on grammar school, I shiver when I remember trying to play softball. When it was my turn to bat, the entire outfield would take three giant steps in. With each of my anemic swings the players encroached even closer, chanting things like "No batter, no batter!"

I still have problems with coordination. The other day I was at a basketball game at Madison Square Garden, and I was sitting next to one of those dumb-ass chronic high-fivers—the guy who gives a high five every time a pass is made. I indulged him as best I could, but I missed his hand just about every time. I think I even hit his lip once. I am just glad my spastic moments were not captured on the Jumbotron for all to see.

On top of everything else, I was also a stutterer. Several friends in my class suffered from the same affliction. Stress exacerbated our condition. When we were alone we were fine, but if we were in the cafeteria and the conversation got a little heated, we would start, to the delight of the other students, to stutter back at each other like a mad pack of farm animals.

When at the Trinity School, an establishment where by the second grade ambitious parents are already trying to get their kids considered for early acceptance to Harvard, by all accounts, I was not making the cut. Eventually, my mother, a kind woman albeit slightly elitist with an upper-class Boston upbringing, was informed that I was "slow." My mother was completely shaken by the news. After all, no one, especially not my society-conscious mother, who had befriended society's finest and who probably would remain dignified during an earthquake, wants a little Forrest Gump running around the house, or, God forbid, the country club. This ignited a frantic search for answers.

Again, I was a Hungerford-Nichols; my ancestors were captains of industry, though granted, they were eventually hung publicly for ruthlessly exploiting the serfs who worked the land. (Really! I found this out when I visited Hungerford Castle, outside of London. There is a plaque outside the ruins that basically calls my ancestors cowards and thieves. Check it out if you are ever in the area.) There must be a solution, specifically a doctor who could put a kinder spin on my "slow" disposition. There was certainly no shortage of "educational experts" out there looking for a buck. Buttressed with my mother's puritanical strength, we set out into the wild labyrinth of the learning-disabled establishment.

If your kid has a learning disability, expect the following. First, in my view no one has a clue about what causes learning disabilities. No doctor or "educational expert" will tell you this. You will hear that the problem is a malfunction in the left brain. Others say that it is a right-brain phenomenon. Others claim that learning disabilities are the result of an inner-ear problem. One doctor actually spun me around in a chair for ten minutes, completely violating my equilibrium, and then asked if I felt dizzy. When I replied "yes," he triumphantly shrieked, "You see!"

Some will say it is an eye problem. Still others subscribe to the theory that learning disabilities are brought on by environmental and sociological conditions. Translation: home life. The most candid doctor, and therefore the least popular, called a spade a spade.

"Look, I think your kid has brain damage. Did you drop him when he was a baby or did he eat a lot of lead paint at some point?" he asked my mother.

Most doctors, however, try to put a positive spin on learning disabilities. After telling the parents, in no uncertain terms, that their son has the reading and writing level of a Neanderthal, they attempt to comfort the parents by telling them that many learning-disabled people are in fact geniuses. They then point out that one of the world's greatest scholars was learning disabled.

"Did you know that Albert Einstein suffered from dyslexia?" the doctors would often ask. Of course, suspecting and hoping that I was a genius, my mother raced me off to yet another doctor to get my IQ tested. To her disappointment, I possessed only an average IQ. I think it would be funny if doctors were more honest and said, "Sure, your son might be a genius. He also might be a total moron, so deal with it." Or better yet, "Mrs. Nichols, I knew Albert Einstein, and your son is no Albert Einstein."

Even as recently as last year, I went to see the most renowned doctor on the East Coast regarding learning disabilities, specifically dyslexia and ADD (I threw in Tourette's for good measure). For a thousand bucks, he gave me a test to see if I had "attention span deficiency." One of the clinical questions on the test was: "Would you have a problem focusing on a documentary about Ben Franklin?" Without hesitation I replied, "Yes. However, I am riveted to a good porno." There is one universal truism: no man has ever had ADD while: a) staring at a vagina, or b) waiting for the card to be turned over on a thousand-dollar hand of blackjack. In both cases, the man is *hyperfocused*.

I told the good doctor, who, judging by the number of toys littering his waiting room, dealt mainly with twelve-year-olds and their parents, that my primary problem was with organization; namely, I had none. Obviously, I kept losing my wallet, keys, and, in short, I was in a state of complete and utter dysfunction. He thought for a moment. He looked pensive, as if he were contemplating having me institutionalized, or at least putting me on some strong meds. Finally, he asked me if I had ever considered using a "fanny pack." I thought about it and realized that even Brad Pitt would look stupid wearing a fanny pack. Unless you happen to be scaling a mountain, a fanny pack looks ridiculous on everyone. When I told him that I was not in any way prepared to sport a fanny pack, he decided to put me on the holistic route to clarity, presenting me with a long list of different herbs and vitamins. He basically sent me out on an herbal scavenger hunt. I could barely get out of bed in the morning, and this guy wanted me to track down shark cartilage.

I felt like saying to him, "Look, I just paid you a thousand bucks, shouldn't you have some shark cartilage on you? Or, at least, write me up a prescription for Ritalin."

Unfortunately, like millions of people, I find myself in the horrible position of being cynical about doctors. I want to like doctors; they are an invaluable asset, and if I ever get hit by a bus I would prefer an MD to an herbalist. Nevertheless, I have had problems with Western medicine's prevailing "take a drug" attitude. Hard to believe, I know.

Anyway, back to my early childhood diagnosis. My mother finally found a medical doctor in Westchester who was willing to diagnose me. Again, this was before ADD/ADHD and dyslexia were household terms. It was not a gentle or trendy diagnosis. The doctor was convinced that because I had tested very poorly across the board she was forced to diagnose me with MBD. *Minimal Brain Dysfunction!!!!!*

I have always suspected that my learning disability might have something to do with the fact that my family, for several years, used to drink out of a pond. There. I said it. We had moved from Manhattan to our weekend house in the country. We had always understood that it was on a spring-fed "lake," yet it had all of the characteristics of a pond, including weeds, algae, and bass. Our water came from a pump house that would push the pond water, via a rusty pipe, up a hill and then through a shoddy filtering system that had the consistency of an Afghan rug. Ten houses surrounded the pond, all of which certainly had leaky septic systems and washing machine discharge pouring into the pond. To compound the problem, on top of one side of the pond was a golf course, which used its share of fertilizers and weed killers that ran into the water.

Sounds like a nice cocktail. My mother may as well have handed my sister and me a big glass of mercury before we got on the school bus. "Here you go! Enjoy your third eye!" Someone, a concerned friend or an environmental enforcement agent, should have stepped in and said something like, "I don't know, maybe you shouldn't be drinking out of this *fucking pond!*"

My mother actually used to try to conceal the aroma of the water, which smelled like it had been filtered through a bass carcass, by adding lemons to it. By the way, I have tangible proof that the pond was hazardous. One of my sisters has MS (or something like it), my stepsister has lupus, I have a severe learning disability and problems pronouncing *th*. And my stepbrother!! My stepbrother married a Jew and moved to Hollywood! (Just kidding.)

Just as with the number of specialists out there, so an unsuspecting person will be shocked by the number of available diagnoses. A friend of mine brought his boy to an "educational expert" (a master's degree in philosophy), who noticed that the boy had a glazed, vacant look to him. This "expert" insisted that my friend immediately take his son to the hospital because he suspected the child was having something called grand mal seizures.

Appropriately terrified, my friend checked his apparently normal kid into a hospital for two days of thorough neurological evaluation. Tests revealed a healthy child.

THE LAST STRAW

Again, in an effort to remain true to my commitment to candor, I must confess that not only was I not a genius, but I also was a little homo. When I was nine years old, I used to make out with boys. I know I am not gay. For starters, I never fantasize about men. Second, throughout my childhood, I never experienced or witnessed an orgasm. I am also positive that there was no oral or anal sex. For, quite frankly, who forgets that?

Here is how it went down. It was basically a combination of poor supervision and budding hormones gone wild. There were three guys with whom I recall messing around. One guy in camp jerked off in front me as he sat perched on top of an inanimate rock in the woods. Another guy I just made out with. My primary "lover" was Tommy, the son of one of my parents' friends. In his apartment, a few blocks away, the grandmotherly babysitter would nod off while watching the popular soap opera *As the World Turns* while we got down to business. Since our only exposure to sex was what we learned watching the soaps, we acted out exactly what we saw on the shows.

For homophobes, skip over this part because I am going to be explicit. First, we made sure that the nanny was in her normal state of dementia in front of the television. Next, we ventured into his parents' bedroom, ripping off each other's clothes and then embraced with passion. Finally, completely naked, we rolled around on the huge king-size bed.

This type of activity is probably a little abnormal. However, that does not bother me. What really pisses me off is that I remember I had these incredible raging erections. My little prick was as hard as a rock for hours it seemed. These days—probably due to years of alcohol and drug abuse coupled with chronic self-abuse (masturbation), not to mention immense amounts of antidepressants cruising through my system at any given time—I have, at best, weak hard-ons, usually alone. In fact, I do not even wake up with one anymore. The grim reality of my sex life is: *My greatest hard-ons were wasted on my male neighborhood friend when I was nine.*

Back then, I was uncertain of my sexual identity. These days, I know I am not gay. I simply do not find men to be sexy. Even if I did, several of my homosexual friends say that my personal hygiene is so deplorable and my skin is so dry that I am unappealing.

My poor, poor mother once caught me and my Tommy locked in an embrace with our tongues jammed down each other's throat. "That is bad!" she said sternly pointing her finger. For her, that was the end of it; she pretended it did not happen. Yet it must have been a traumatizing event. This sort of behavior, along with the fact that I could not read or write and the fact that I had a voracious appetite for mood-altering substances, was more than my parents could bear.

ROLLING HILLS AND BONG HITS

In 1976, brochures for what we'll call "Wickendon School" were quite impressive. There were pictures of large colonial mansions in an idyllic New England setting, replete with imperial, sparkling white pillars, and focused, clean-cut preps riveted to teachers in tutoring sessions. There were other pictures of peppy preps enjoying their innocence while skiing, hiking, and playing in the NBA-quality gymnasium. Besides the pictures, testimonials praised the one-to-seven teacher-student ratio. The brochure also implied that each student would be sent to some mainstream institution like Choate or Deerfield after finishing Wickendon. The brochure certainly substantiated the $20,000 annual tuition.

Having attended Wickendon, I am convinced that 80 percent of the tuition money went into the brochure. That brochure deserved a marketing award. There was no gymnasium on campus. The gym in the brochure was the local YMCA. The actual campus had only one main building with a bunch of cheap annexes attached to it. The other buildings were trailers converted into classrooms. One building was called the "chicken coop" because that is what it once had been. (I will admit it had been significantly remodeled since the chickens flew the coop.)

Although there were some dedicated teachers at Wickendon, I found most of them to be young, poorly trained, and apathetic. What the brochure did was lure parents in, and then the headmaster, nothing if not an astute salesperson, would snow them so well that they would not realize that the campus actually resembled a Pakistani refugee camp.

One of Wickendon's most popular sport was skiing. When the school's van showed up at the mountain, all took notice. I find it remarkable that kids who were supposed to have attention span problems remained completely focused on shooting spitballs and generally making the trip an absolute nightmare for the poor driver, who constantly put on the blinker, pulled over, and screamed, "You kids suck!"

Someone was always up to mischief. Once, a kid pissed in a

cup and passed it around to the other kids in the van. Each kid was terrified of spilling it—until one finally did. That kid was laughed at mercilessly and then ostracized. He spent five hours with someone else's urine on him.

For even the normal person, buying lift tickets, renting skis, and locating mittens can create sensory overload. For Wickendon students, it was complete and utter chaos.

"I forgot one ski!"

"Where's my mitten?"

"I can't find my hat!"

At the mountain, most counselors and teachers simply tuned us out as we wandered off, leaving a trail of poles, tickets, clothing, mittens, and skis in our wake.

Not everyone was a mess, however. Some kids looked spectacular on the slopes. Adorned in the best equipment money could buy, these kids made it down the slope in perfect parallel form in their expensive sweaters and designer sunglasses. I, on the other hand, looked like a monstrosity coming down the slope. I wore one of those big green snorkel jackets with fur on the front of the hood and orange on the back. I would always purchase one of those hideous suede face masks. Upon the second run down the bunny slope, I would have snot running down the side of my face mask, and my ass crack would be completely exposed, chafed, and red from my wiping out several hundred times. Forced to rent equipment, my rental boots were black with huge conspicuous numbers painted in white on the back, resembling something a prisoner would wear: 186 right, 186 left . . . go get 'em Franz. At the end of the day, no one was sober enough to make out the numbers. Just about every student was stoned, drunk, or crying.

While I did not learn much, I did meet a fleet of characters. One was Gary, who hailed from Massapequa, Long Island. At three hundred pounds, he had a huge square Fred Flintstone–type head perched on his large frame. Gary had greasy skin, wore only polyester, and had a great sense of humor. Students were always trying to get him riled. One of the most effective ways was to mock his hometown by saying it three times, then adding the word *penis* to the end: Massapequa, Massapequa, Massapequa-penis. At this, Gary would erupt and attempt to strangle his closest tormentor, but invariably Gary was too slow to capture his giggling adolescent nemesis.

Gary, like most of us, was an enigma. On a superficial level, one would not suspect that Gary had intellectual aptitude or critical thinking skills. He was sheepish, inarticulate, and prone to wringing his hands over and over. A closer look at Gary would reveal much more. Gary was an accomplished artist who drew with remarkable detail and accuracy. His art was tangible testimony to his intelligence; a more subtle form was Gary's sense of humor.

It was almost as if he were in on a cosmic joke. For example, an annex of the student lounge was really nothing more than a crawl space, but it was big enough to accommodate Gary's considerable mass. My classmates and I would equip Gary with a flashlight and station him in the back of the space. Next, we would solicit an unsuspecting student, often female, to enter the front of the room claiming that there was some "great stuff back there." We would then close the door, leaving the person in complete darkness. On cue Gary would flash the light underneath his tremendous head and lumber toward the screeching onlooker, who would inevitably pound at the door relentlessly before getting released, convulsing with laughter. Gary had a wonderful theatrical quality that was a sure sign of intelligence, a form of intelligence that, regrettably, would never show up on a standardized test.

Then there was Raymond, a wealthy French kid. Raymond was short with light skin. He had a strong but stubby body and was completely uncoordinated. I believe one of his legs was longer than the other. Shorter than his diminutive physique was his temper. Raymond's combination of a quirky disposition, cultural idiosyncrasy, and ability to lose his temper to the point of foaming at the mouth made him an easy and desirable target. Most of the pranks played on Raymond were annoying but benign, things like short-sheeting his bed, putting toothpaste in his Gucci loafers, inserting peeled fruit at the bottom of his bed, or simply knocking his books out of his hands. Other times, we came up with more elaborate methods of provoking him, like the time a few of us climbed onto the rafters above his bed and dripped water down on him. We would go to great lengths to get the coveted tantrums we so loved to watch. Other attacks were violent, such as the time we pelted Raymond with ice balls, or barricaded him in his closet. Like Gary, Raymond was uncoordinated but strong as an ox. You certainly would not want Raymond to get ahold of you. He had a very powerful grip (what we called "retard strength") and was known to bite. However, he was very easily eluded. When Raymond attempted to grab a tormentor, he would often miss and wind up falling to the ground, which further compounded his rage. The young teachers, many of whom smoked pot on campus, did not help matters. They also seemed to enjoy Raymond's tantrums. Even the good-hearted teachers failed to put their foot down. To my astonishment, they would often blame poor Raymond for our assaults on him.

"Raymond," they would say, "these boys like the way you react. If you wouldn't react that way, they wouldn't pick on you." We were putting toothpaste in his shoes! How was he supposed to react? Like Gandhi? The principal simply should have sat us all down and said, "The next kid who picks on Raymond in any way will be publicly flogged!"

Wickendon mandated that all students play a sport. On parents' weekend, we were to showcase the talents we had learned and cultivated all semester. Basically, it was a chance for them to see their twenty grand at work. I was a part of the treasured equestrian program. In addition to the brochure, the school actually did dump a lot of cash into horseback riding. There was an indoor riding ring, many well-bred horses, and a top-notch British instructor dedicated to teaching equally dedicated riders (she was completely hot).

I signed up for the program not because I was interested but because I had heard through the degenerate grapevine that it was a blow-off sport. The instructor had no patience or interest in helping apathetic pot smokers such as myself, and I was relegated to the field and trail class, which was an underachiever's oasis. It was a blast. We took our horses out to the rolling fields and basically got stoned and drunk. Since no one knew a thing about horses or riding, we were given the stable's worst steeds. These horses hated us for our ignorance as well as occasionally blowing bong hits up their snouts. God, what little assholes we were. Often, in disgust, the horses simply stopped short and sent unsuspecting pothead degenerate riders onto the rock-hard ground. On our little journeys, we made forts, had rock fights, and got high before walking the horses back to campus two hours later. Three of us had such bad ADD that we never even managed to grasp the basic concept of how to saddle a horse. We paid one kid with pot to saddle the horses for the rest of us. At any rate, parents' weekend was rapidly approaching, and I had to participate in the horse show, a terrifying thought.

Going AWOL meant no weekend mall trips. What could I do during the riding show? Blow smoke up the horse's snout? I couldn't even put a saddle on. Why couldn't I have signed up for JV soccer, where I could have simply waved enthusiastically to my parents from my cozy seat on the bench? Two days before the event, I desperately tried to acquaint myself with the fundamentals of riding, like how to trot, but I could not get the instructor's attention. She was too busy helping her star pupils fine-tune their programs.

On the day of the show, a crowd of what must have been two hundred people circled the riding ring. The pressure was on. First, I tried in vain to establish a rapport with my designated beast. I offered a carrot and hoped he had forgotten the way I had treated the poor thing. Meanwhile, I heard the enthusiastic applause for other groups that were doing well. I searched for the guy who usually helped me put on the saddle, but he was nowhere to be found. I tried appealing to the instructor for help. Ultimately, I had to buckle the saddle myself. I was so fat and out of shape that I could not even mount up. Finally, showing disgust bordering on hatred, the riding instructor gave me a leg up.

My event, the field and trail showcase, was relatively simple.

Unlike previous classes, I was to be spared major jumps and can-
tering. All I had to do was walk the horse around the ring, step
over a few two-foot logs, trot a bit, grab a raincoat off a fence,
and circle the ring one more time. Prior to the show, I was told
that since only three kids dared to show up for my event, I was
guaranteed a medal if I completed the course. While still terrified, I was inspired by the thought of receiving an award for
the first time in my life. To my chagrin, competitors who went
before me did okay. Finally, it was my turn. As the instructor
led me and my angry, old, uncooperative horse out into the
ring, I heard chuckles from the crowd. I was a fat little fuck
in my black Ted Nugent concert T-shirt, which, incidentally,
failed to conceal my fleshy love handles. Plus, I never wore a
belt, and much of my backside was exposed (plumbers' butt),
but this was the least of my worries. I was so nervous I thought
I would shit spaghetti.

To start the program, I nudged the horse, kicking it once. I
don't know if the horse refused out of revenge or if it had simply
grown immune to the many drunken kicks I had administered
in the woods, but it simply would not move. The crowd chuck-
led louder. I kicked harder but still got no reaction from the
horse. While many were still laughing, others were angry.

"That's abusive!" someone bellowed. But I didn't care. In an
act of desperation, I took the crop, which was intended primarily for ornamental purposes, and began violently smacking the
stubborn old beast while frantically kicking its side. I always
had pretty weak legs and I don't think I was really harming or
hurting the horse, but now most onlookers booed and hollered
in protest. Finally, just before I was sure to be disqualified, the
horse labored toward the obstacle course.

"Please, horse, just step over the logs," I said to myself. Being that there were only three people in my group, I actually thought I might be able to snag a medal. However, the horse stopped short at the first log and sent me lunging forward, hitting my chin on the horse's neck. Now the crowd was back to laughing uncontrollably. I kept my head down, praying not to catch my father's eyes. My greatest fear was that someone would yell out: "Whose kid is that?" I was allowed one more attempt. I backtracked. Miraculously, the horse cooperated and even broke into a trot. However, it then proceeded to topple every log that we went over. This once again invoked howls from the crowd. For each log knocked over, seven points were deducted. Even so, I was still eligible for a medal. I just had to grab a rain slicker off a post. My first attempt was a failure. After a few agonizing minutes, I managed to negotiate the horse closer so that I could reach the elusive slicker. The coat was in my grasp, but I dropped it.

"Aaaaaawwww," the crowd groaned. All was not lost, though. According to the rules, I was allowed to dismount, pick up the slicker, and take the final lap. With slicker in hand, I attempted to mount the horse. However, I hadn't secured the saddle tightly and as I attempted to mount, the saddle slid off. I was disqualified. I was ordered out of the ring, ineligible for even third place. Maybe I should have simply blown pot smoke into the horse's face.

I was caught smoking pot a couple of times during my stay at Wickendon and managed to talk my way out each time. Just as a blind person will develop other senses, a learning-disabled kid will learn to bullshit. I remember getting busted by a dean who observed smoke lingering in a bathroom my friends and I had just exited. Searching our pockets, the dean found rolling papers. Luckily, there was no pot to be found, for we had finished our stash and flushed the roach.

Waiting for our hearing, my posse was near tears. "Listen to me!" I commanded, "We were not getting high. We were smoking cigarettes—a much lesser violation and penalty! Pull yourselves together. When we get into the office do not say a word. Let me do the talking!" I did what lawyers do: Deny, deny, counter-accuse!

I cannot recall what I told the committee, but I had to be a rather spectacular performance. To the outrage and humiliation of the dean who had clearly caught us, I managed to get us all off under some "inconclusive evidence" clause. I had such confidence back then. If I could summon 10 percent of the confidence I used to have, I would be happy today.

The summer after Wickendon I attended what was ostensibly a sailing camp for boys with special needs. The first day there I was reminded that "special needs" had a wide umbrella. I remember waking up the first morning to find that the kid in the bunk next to me was putting on my sneakers.

"What are you, retarded?" I asked him sarcastically.

"A little bit," he replied.

NExT!

After two years at Wickendon, my parents and I set off to find another boarding school. While I had some degenerate character traits and some questionable ethics, I yearned to be a part of the establishment. My friends at home were super-preppy, and I embraced it completely. I loved wearing pink and green madras or *Nantucket reds*. I would have preferred attending some prestigious prep school like Exeter, but, with my learning disability, those highly selective institutions were not an option. Instead, I chose a school with the most attractive campus that would accept me as long as my family could pony up the loot.

Though lacking sports facilities, the Forman School in Litchfield, Connecticut, was absolutely magnificent. The Berkshire hills were visible from the school, which was perched atop a hill. I loved Forman. There was a real progressive energy on the campus, and the majority of teachers were on the ball. Just a few years earlier, Forman had been a cesspool of stoners who liked to screw and screw up. Now, the new headmaster and his wife had reinvigorated the school and its staff. The headmaster's wife, Mrs. Pierce, managed to get even the most LD kid interested in reading and comprehending Shakespeare. The math teacher, Mrs. Pavlac, a Yale graduate, would work one-on-one with students. She could make a student understand algebra in under an hour. These educators' hard work paid off: 85 percent of my graduating class went to college. They also had great tutors at Forman, and it was amazing how much a good, inspired tutor could help a student. My parents hired Mrs. Pavlac at twenty dollars an hour and she single-handedly got me through algebra two.

Forman had all the trappings of a real prep school. We even had a debating team, and I was on it. Unfortunately, the only other schools that had debating teams were places like Andover and Exeter. The unrealistically optimistic debating coach,

Mr. Becker, would pile a bunch of misfit illiterates, many of us plagued with mild to severe speech impediments, into a van and off we would go for a five-hour drive up to New England, only to get absolutely demolished by the competition.

Despite its academic success, Forman did have its share of troubles. Specifically, the students loved to get high. This was something Mr. Pierce tried desperately to correct.

"It's the five percent! That five percent ruins the quality of life for everyone else on this campus!" he preached, referring to those who used booze and did drugs. Little did Mr. Pierce know that it was probably closer to 95 percent. Like many boarding school kids, students were obsessed with sneaking booze and drugs onto campus and would use any apparatus at their disposal.

Like a lot of kids at most boarding schools across the country, students shoved pot into the shaft of a lacrosse stick, hid pot and other assorted drugs in the backs of radios and lamps. So how did I distinguish myself in this crowd? Once, I remember using a Flex shampoo bottle to sneak in some booze. I took the empty bottle, which I had found in the trash at my parents' house, and filled it with samples from each bottle of my parents' liquor cabinet. We called this "monkey piss." With my degenerate friends in the dorm basement, I opened the bottle and foam seeped over the sides.

"Oooh," the guys let out.

"Fellas, it's not what it looks like or tastes like that matters, it's what it does to you!" I told them. Repulsed, they stepped back as I started to guzzle the concoction and suds seeped down the sides of my mouth.

Like all good delinquents, we did not always rely on conventional measures to escape from reality. Most of the students came from wealthy families and therefore had charge accounts at the bookstore. Though it seems unbelievable today, back then we were allowed to charge cigarettes to our accounts. I would say conservatively that 90 percent of the student body smoked. Worse than the cigarette pandemic was the Wite-Out correcting fluid craze. One kid figured out that it was possible to get a "buzz" snorting Wite-Out. Word spread and the bookstore was fresh out of Wite-Out only a few days later.

Forman claimed to be at the forefront of helping kids who learn "differently," and it was not all talk. Someone in the administration got the idea to let the kids with LD take the SAT untimed. It was approved by the powers that be, and the year I took the SAT, I had no time limit. What the administration overlooked was that even with no limit LD kids, myself included, would hand in their answer sheets and take off only an hour into taking the exam.

In an effort to help develop students' vocabulary for this very test, some Forman administrators came up with the "Word of the Day." During lunchtime announcements in the cafeteria, one student from a designated table was to announce a word, give a definition, and then use it in a sentence. While the pedagogical approach to expose students to new SAT words was good in theory, it was ultimately ineffective in practice, mainly due to the fact that no one listened, and it was an irresistible target for sabotage. Six weeks into the Word of the Day exercise, Stuart, a normally quiet, sheepish kid who for some reason hung with the tough kids, stood up proudly, and pulled out an index card.

"The word of the day is *vagina*," he announced very deliberately and clearly. Forman's student body broke into hysterics. Even the teachers, many in their twenties, had difficulty fighting back the laughs. The older teachers and administrators were not amused. However, their protests of "Good God!" and "Outrageous!" were drowned out by the chorus of hysterical teenagers.

"The vagina is an organ that houses the clitoris . . ." he continued matter-of-factly. He then talked graphically of walls, lips, and cavities, all the while sticking diligently to the Word of the Day format.

"My girlfriend has a big, stinking—" Before he could get out the last word, a brigade of male teachers tackled Stuart. It was too late, though. The damage had been done. We all roared and cheered. At this point, there was no way anyone could contain us.

The next day, the headmaster made a stern announcement.

"The Word of the Day is *judgment*. Stuart used incredibly poor judgment, and for this he has been suspended." Forman's finest were now silent and solemn. The headmaster was certain that other people had put Stuart up to it, probably the 5 percent, and he was determined to seek them out and punish them to the fullest extent of the Forman bylaws.

"Also," he added, "There will be no more Word of the Day, due to the 'five percent.'"

Being a little addict, every time I went home to New York and visited a friend, I raided the parents' medicine cabinet. One time I stumbled upon a delightful little psychostimulant called Dexedrine, an amphetamine often prescribed for ADD, and helped myself to a generous handful.

Back at school, I took one little nugget of productivity every morning. I recall some of my spontaneous humor and genuine good nature may have been tempered, but I also believe my study habits were certainly enhanced. I was actually, without knowing it, self-medicating for ADD.

FAT, DRUNK, AND STUPID

It is said that George Bush is dyslexic. He thrived socially at Yale while leaning heavily on his friends for academic help. I have heard that, like many learning-disabled people, George relied heavily on booze as a social lubricant.

Despite poor results on standardized tests, I actually managed to get into a fairly competitive college. I remember my interview at Hobart in Geneva, New York. A pleasant, attractive, healthy young woman inquired about my SAT scores. Embarrassed by my poor performance, I told her that standardized tests were not partial to dyslexics and therefore my scores were not my strongest assets. I went on to mention my other strengths in sports and extracurricular activities. This only perked her interest more. People want to hear numbers, it's that simple.

"Oh, come. I'm sure that they were not that bad, you seem like a smart guy, how bad could they be?" the admissions lady protested, not unpleasantly. We badgered back and forth and finally I yielded to her relentless prodding.

"Four-eighty," I confessed bleakly.

"Look, it's certainly not great, but I have heard of much worse. Now, did you get that score in math or English?" Then the moment of shame was upon me; I told her that it was a combined score. She must have liked me or liked that I was a Nichols or liked that I could ante up the twenty-five grand a year. Maybe she thought I could become a good alumnus if I managed to graduate. Who knows why I got in, but I did.

Hobart represented total emancipation for me. Free from the restrictions of boarding school rules, I could drink as much as I wanted, whenever I wanted. The inherent problem with Hobart, like most upstate schools, was that cornfields surround it. Here's a warning to any parent: if the school is in a cornfield, drinking is epidemic. Basically, parents are paying at least thirty thousand dollars a year so their kids can drink beer and try to fuck. Remember the drinking age was eighteen in 1985. If I recall correctly, during orientation weekend an industrial beer truck drove onto the quad where all the freshmen sat around getting shit-faced before staggering back to the dorm to try to have sex.

As was the case at a lot of schools, alcohol abuse was rampant on campus. One of the first nights there, a bunch of guys were in front of my dorm room sitting around a large garbage can. One guy was mixing up some concoction with a lacrosse stick as a couple of others poured in an array of beverages. Girls were conspicuously absent from the gathering. This was no weekend social gathering; it was no cocktail party. These guys were "industrial drinking" in the middle of the week just to get drunk. One guy had already vomited in the corner and no one seemed to mind. Unlike young women, who at that age make a huge production when one of them gets sick, guys have no problem with projectile vomiting. I approached with caution and noticed that they all had red mouths and were drinking out of metal Hi-C containers with jagged edges. One of the crew ordered me to go find a cup, and I got my water glass from my room. When I reemerged, cup in hand, these hooligans laughed at me hysterically. Apparently, my 12-ounce Hobart lacrosse cup was an insult to the others who were guzzling from quart-sized cans. I loved to party, but I thought that guzzling with these animals might actually be dangerous—and I had class the next morning. One pie-eyed drunk informed me that the main ingredient to the concoction they were brewing was grain alcohol. Earlier that day someone had driven to a moonshine operation in Pennsylvania and brought back an ample supply.

Some guy gave me a larger container and demanded that I chug. As I drank, I threw all caution to the wind. Two minutes after the drink hit me, I started to feel loose, strong, and athletic. These lacrosse brutes no longer intimidated me. Five minutes later, I was no longer meek. I was in charge.

"If you want to get a real buzz, you need to eat the fruit that absorbs the alcohol too," I instructed. (Fruit absorbs alcohol.) As the alcohol worked its magic, all inhibitions vanished. I had arrived. I felt omnipotent. All my fears of not fitting in vanished. I knew I could be very popular at Hobart.

My step-brother, Mike, who went to Boston University, a party school in its own right, readily confesses that his three most drunken experiences were had at Hobart. As far as beer, Hobart's undergrads preferred just good old plain keg beer with names like Milwaukee's Best, Genny Light, Genny Cream Ale, Pabst Blue Ribbon. (Pabst Blue Ribbon beer tasted so bad I can't imagine what ranked worse. I remember riding shotgun next to my good friend Ed and drinking a case on our drive back up to school.)

Timing is everything in life. Unlike in the previous decades, in the '80s there were no discos and little political activism on campus. Instead, students had John Belushi. It so happened that I attended college only four years after *National Lampoon's Animal House* was released. Fat, drunk, and stupid was in. When I tell my friends today how much I drank at Hobart, they all say "Who didn't?" As if their colleges were like Hobart—I am not convinced that they do know: I think that the consumption was too astronomical to comprehend . . . really.

I lived the Animal House experience. In fact, I hid in the fraternity system, pledging Theta Delta Chi, the party frat. At the time I attended college, fraternities were at their peak across the United States. Everyone sported Benetton rugby shirts and got drunk at toga parties. The sole purpose of drinking was to get drunk, and at Hobart it seemed sanctioned by the university itself: official student activities sponsored by various departments had kegs, and every dorm floor had at least one or two beer funnels. The frat system gave me self-esteem, however illegitimate and unhealthy. I was a partyer, goddamnit. It was a lot of fun, quite frankly.

In 1984 there was no real formal grading at Hobart. There were grades, but if you did not like your grade you could take a "slash," meaning the grade would not affect your GPA. When I arrived on campus in the fall of 1984, there were students who had been there for ten years.

Today, if you overheard a group of NYU students talking about pulling an "all-nighter," odds are they would be referring to getting some coffee and studying all night. In my circles at Hobart, the only ingredients we needed for an all-nighter were a keg of beer, some blow, and a couple of sheep.

People in my circles were not interested in academics. They

were, however, interested in "blacking out." Blacking out meant that we consumed so much booze that we did not know what we had done the night before. This is still common on campuses today, but what made Hobart special was that we did it seven days a week. Every morning my frat brothers and I would congregate over breakfast and determine at what point we had each blacked out or begun to "brown out."

Meeting women was never a priority in my circles. A fraternity member would merely drink all night and whatever he came home with is what he got. There were exceptions sometimes when it came to picking up girls at parties, but only one rule: "Go ugly early and avoid the rush."

The down side to my college experience was that my entire identity was based on being a party animal. Because I looked a little like Sean Penn, I was instantly anointed with the name Spicoli (the burnout character from *Fast Times at Ridgemont High*). It was tough to shake. Another one of my nicknames was "Iron Lung," which I earned by being able to inhale an immense amount of pot from a four-foot skull bong without coughing. It's funny how one thing could make you popular in one place and not necessarily help you in another down the line.

"What are your strengths and weaknesses?" interviewers asked after college.

"Well, I don't speak too well, but I brought this bong along to demonstrate my lung strength. You got a light?"

The irony is that while I smoked pot every day at Hobart, I hated it. I hated the feeling of being stoned. I liked the trappings—the paraphernalia, the bongs, the zip-locking bags, the buds, the smell, the camaraderie. I liked buying the stuff, and I liked having a big bag. I liked being bad. But the feeling of being stoned was of displacement and subtle paranoia. Yet I smoked every day. I don't know how that stuff calms people down.

Once, and only once, I invited a high school buddy up to visit. The relatively small three-foot bong got passed to him and he did the unthinkable—he coughed; he choked on the smoke! Not only that, water went out of the bowl and onto the floor. He may as well have taken a shit on the carpet. I was embarrassed. My friends looked at me with contempt; how could I?

At Hobart I remember a class called Critical Thinking 101. Its objective was to encourage students to, well, to think critically. I have to admit that the tenets of the class did pay off, for I did begin to think "critically." I would be in my dorm room at night and be like, "You know what? I think this bag of pot is definitely smaller than the bag of pot that I bought last week. I am very critical of this."

What got me into real trouble were hard drugs. At first, I started doing drugs to supplement my drinking. If I wanted to party three days straight without sleep, drugs would help me.

Somewhere during my sophomore year, I was introduced to ecstasy. Every weekend, my friends—when I say "friends," I mean anyone who I could find who wanted to do drugs—and I would do it. One time, a friend and I got hold of close to an ounce of ecstasy and we snorted the entire bag in one night. I was sick for days and shook for weeks afterward. Ecstasy aged me severely. You know that feeling when you wake up and feel Tony-the-Tiger great? You smell everything and your senses are alive. Well *adios* to that! I also physically felt creaky at twenty-one years old. Since that night, life has never been the same for me. I have moments of happiness, spots of clarity, but the sustained happiness and sense of well-being that I had as a kid has left me. Sometimes, I try to simulate those feelings with massive amounts of coffee, but it is not really the same. Of course, exercise helps get the serotonin levels up.

I feel it is important to state that I believe hard drugs like acid and ecstasy gave me long-term "glitches" (fear of certain numbers/symbols) that temper my happiness—and that of everyone near me. I would not wish the long-term paranoia and torment associated with massive ecstasy abuse on even my worst enemy. Well, maybe Bin Laden and friends could have a little, fuck them.

As far as neurological impact, I have learned that there is nothing more corrosive than ecstasy. A doctor once told me that what I did to my brain that night was worse than what a junkie does to his brain after using heroin for twenty years.

When I came home from college on breaks, like most kids who abuse ecstasy, I was depressed and paranoid. Tough to be around. I thought of suicide often; somehow I got through that hard period, but believe me, I tormented my family and friends with mood swings and mania. I simply could not make a decision. I would start to do one thing and abort that and do something else. One time I drove from New York to Boston to see a Grateful Dead concert, got to the stadium, and turned around and came home.

Sports were revered at Hobart. It had an incredible lacrosse team that went undefeated for years. I think. (Truthfully, I was always in the parking lot getting my sway on. I believe I saw only one game.) Partying was as respected as sports. Therefore, I, as well as others in search of an identity, thought that the more I drank, the more popular I would be. Twice I was sent to the hospital with alcohol poisoning.

I would go to any level to shock my peers. I would drink beer out of a filthy puddle on the floor, sleep with anybody, and drive my Jeep all over campus without ever going near a road. (I hit a swimming pool once.)

I used to love to walk completely naked from my room in the frat into a crowded party (three hundred people), my shriveled little penis barely visible, high as a kite bellowing: "Who's got blow? Anyone got blow? Who's got coke?" Then I would watch the place clear out like someone let loose a skunk.

My greatest effort at grossness, at least that I can remember, was one warm spring night when I went up to a screen door where hundreds of buzzing, snapping insects had been drawn by the light. To the dismay of onlookers, I ate every single bug on that screen. Some went down harder than others. As I recall, the large beetles offered the most resistance, while the moths went quietly. Today, when I see people eating bugs on *The Howard Stern Show* and *Fear Factor*, I take some pride in the fact that I was a pioneer in the field of bug eating.

Finally, there was a place called the quarry where students would go to swim illegally and hang out. There were a couple of ledges from which people would jump in, provided they missed the rusty old cars that were submerged in the shallow water. In a desperate attempt to distinguish myself and display my latent athleticism, I would climb to the top of the highest peak and hurl myself off, doing spastic flips in the air. I was told that one time I somehow pulled off two and a half flips. The people below found it to be extremely entertaining, and I liked to challenge the best athlete to match me. Most did not rise to the occasion. Had I found my niche, or was this simply the "Evel Knievel syndrome"?

Like a lot of insecure guys, I hid in the empowering womb of the frat house. As artificial as it was, the frat had become my identity, and there was power in numbers. One of my least proud experiences reveals how being in a frat house can fuel one's ego to such an extent that he becomes destructive.

Of the plethora of absurdities that the Greek system has to offer, the most ridiculous is how most fraternities and sororities have a stricter social code than the US military. One evening I polished off an entire bottle of tequila with my friend, Bill Evans, which we did every Wednesday night. Afterward I decided to go out on a solo rampage. I was bar hopping on my own and looking for trouble. I was not necessarily a good fighter or a big guy, but for some reason, when I was on tequila all bets were off. Even the football players kept their distance. I was not sure whether they saw the violence in my eye or they were simply afraid that I would vomit on them. Either way, they gave me a wide berth.

I recall staggering home angry and horny when I heard a party going on in a neighboring frat house. I went in looking for love. After being curtly rejected by every girl I approached, my eyes fell upon a fraternity pledge of mine who was dancing and having a great time with not one, but two girls. He was happy and buoyant; I was sullen and trashed. Now, there is a strict rule in the fraternity system that prohibits pledges from attending rival fraternity parties. I approached the guy and told him that he should leave. Then I went to annoy some other people. When I returned to the dance floor, to my amazement and rage, I saw that the pledge had disregarded my orders and was still dancing. Keep in mind that if I were dancing with a pretty girl myself, I would have had no problem with his being there. But that was not the case. I was not getting any action. In fact, girls were looking at my sorry ass with disdain. Therefore, this poor pledge was about to receive some misdirected sexual frustration. I went up to him on the dance floor, grabbed him by the collar, pulled him out on the porch, and told him to leave again. At this point, although my request was absurd and sick, he probably should have listened to me and taken his group elsewhere. Instead, he said something to me like "Why do have to be such a dick?" (Good point.) I simple grabbed him and threw him down a flight of stairs like it was nothing.

The next day at something like seven a.m., the time when the pledges assembled to clean the house, I went out to the pledge line where all fifty guys were being screamed at and humiliated in various ways. When I approached the pledge with whom I'd had the incident, I noticed that he had a big cut on his eye and his arm was in a sling.

It turned out that I had broken his arm and he needed some stitches above his eye. Worse than the significant injuries was the dialogue, or lack thereof, that followed. When I approached him, he told me that he had been out of line and that it would not happen again. I laughed and told him that it had better not. That was the end of it. I had thrown this kid down a flight of stairs and could have easily killed him, and he was apologizing to me.

The guy did have his revenge on some level. Years later I bumped into him on the street. He had a beautiful girl with him, and I must have looked like a deranged homeless guy. He did not yell at me. Far worse, he simply ignored me. I would submit that, while there were some good guys in the fraternities, most of us ran to the frat houses for our identities and safety.

My behavior became more embarrassing when my sweet cousin Betsy decided to follow family tradition and attend Hobart. (Her father, my uncle, also went there.) This was my drinking kingdom. Now I would have to alter my behavior and have some accountability? Luckily, she was cool. She was pleased to see me.

Speaking of altered, one time I decided it would be a good idea to take a hit of acid in the middle of the crowded stands at a football game. Not advisable. I was freaked out. I thought the players were melting and my friends, knowing that I had taken acid, began to torment me. In a state of unspeakable anxiety I made my way in haste for the exit.

All I wanted was to get to nature, to the safe haven of a lake or the woods, anything to get my head together. (As anyone who has taken acid knows, crowds or places like McDonald's are where you simply do not want to be. You also do not want to try to pick up chicks, incidentally.) At any rate, I was desperately trying to get through the maze of tailgaters in the parking lot, when I heard my name: "Jeffrey! Jeffrey!" I looked up to see my cousin skipping buoyantly toward me. She was so genuinely glad to see me it hurt. I did not have the heart to tell her I was tripping my balls off.

So we started to engage in small talk. We bantered back and forth about her heavy course load and how our uncle Art was doing. During the conversation I mindlessly fiddled with a hood ornament on a car. The more nervous I got (at one point I believe my sweet cousin appeared to have three heads) the more I twisted and pulled at this hood ornament. I believe it was a huge greyhound or lion or something. Finally, I twisted the thing so hard that it broke off in my fucking hand.

I yelled. My cousin yelled. Worst of all, the owner of the vehicle, who was "tailgating" at the other end of the station wagon, yelled.

"What the fuck!" he screamed. He was a huge townie guy. Even under the influence of a heavy hallucinogenic I was still a good bullshitter. Actually, it was not even bullshit that came out of my mouth. It was the truth.

As my cousin looked on in absolute shock, I told the guy, whose fists were clenched and ready to unload years of brewing animosity toward college kids, that it was a total mistake and I was nervous because I was tripping on acid. I promised with genuine feeling that I would pay to have it fixed, and I took down the guy's number. To this day, I regret that I misplaced the number and was never able to make good on my promise. He has probably pummeled some other poor unsuspecting college kid because of me.

One enlightening moment I had at Hobart occurred on my second day on campus. I did not want to sit with the other loser freshmen in my dorm. I knew with that crew I could never pick up any girls, so I went off to sit by myself. It looked like my experiment paid off when a beautiful girl came up to my table, pointed to a chair, and asked me kindly if anyone was sitting there. I remember thinking college is going to be great. Yahoo!

"No. Please, it's all yours," I told her. To my dismay, she thanked me, pulled out the chair, and brought it over to her friends.

How did I get through college? I can only believe that I was pretty good at getting the gist of things. Forman had done its job of teaching me how to write the five-paragraph essay (intro, body, conclusion, or something like that), and I cheated my ass off.

I do not want to completely marginalize my college experience. It was a lot fun, and there were some good people up in that cornfield, but it certainly screwed me up. The sad thing about being a party animal in college is that those years are critical developmental years. Essentially, I learned how to be a bum.

And, let's face it, the fraternity system in general (thank God, most of the worst of them have been shut down) breeds racism, sexism, and certainly alcoholism. I fear fraternities have scarred many people. The only thing they do not breed are brain cells.

AND THEN THERE WERE NONE

I know I have been throwing the word *burnout* around loosely, but maybe now I should take a moment to talk about brain cells; specifically, how I got rid of so many. Indulge me in some simple math: most of us (supposedly) are born with billions of healthy, active, vibrant neurons, all playfully dancing around in the mind's universe. Then the addict in us, around the age of five, starts to knock them off little by little.

As a tiny child, do you recall spinning around until you got dizzy and fell down? There go a couple of thousand. Let's jump ahead now to preadolescent years. What about hyperventilating—where one kid crouches in the corner, then stands up to have his predegenerate friend squeeze the air out of him until he gets so light-headed he almost passes out? There go a couple of thousand more neurons. Whippets, Rush, and Wite-Out. One million neurons. At sixteen there is booze, pot, mushrooms, acid, and cocaine. There go a couple more million. Then, Valium and painkillers, and a couple more thousand disappear. This is no problem; there are still millions of neurons left, and we only use 10 percent of our brain anyway.

But then the designer drugs come in. Ecstasy. Special K. Crack. These wipe out hemispheres of active brain cells. Massive colonies are destroyed. Whole cities lost.

Acid. Now, acid is brutal on the mind, though undeniably enlightening. There must be many acid casualties locked up in psych wards. When I was on acid, I saw all the problems of the world very clearly. My senses were heightened, and I felt more in touch with nature and the universe. You saw capitalism for what it was: mainly the destruction of natural resources in the name of commerce. Corporate greed and exploitation/marketing jumps out at you with the same power as someone sticking a thumb up your ass. "You really get it, man!" How could such clarity be bad? The problem was the next day I could barely tie my shoe. Mushrooms were pretty bad, too. I probably had twenty mushroom trips. They were absolute blasts. All I did was laugh (mushrooms didn't make me as introspective as acid). However, I do not think the mind ever fully recovers from a bad acid or mushroom trip.

For these reasons, I no longer do drugs or alcohol. Using simple math, I have two brain cells left, and I am going to take care of them, goddamnit! I actually had an MRI done on my brain once, and the doctor told me, rather sheepishly, that I actually had no brain.

Of all the drugs out there, ecstasy is the most corrosive to the brain. Through years of attending AA meetings I know that many celebrities have been sidelined from abusing this drug. It is a shame they do not go public about it. The good news is that the brain has a way of healing itself and it can create new electrical pathways—if you are lucky.

OFF TO EUROPE

As difficult as learning disabilities are for the individual who has them, they are even worse on the unfortunate people who have to deal with that individual. My bicycle trip across Europe illustrates this point.

I was beat after college. As I have established, probably ad nauseam, I had spent four years druggin', drinkin', and blastin' some serious crap up my nose. Everyone needs their brain cells, but LD people need them more than most. We have no business playing around with brain-damaging substances.

So after college, not only did I have ADD and dyslexia, but I was a burnout to boot. (Let's just say that I was a "little light on dopamine." Dopamine is a hormone and neurotransmitter produced in the brain. It is associated with concentration and euphoria among other things, and insufficient levels of dopamine are the main culprit for many of the symptoms of Parkinson's disease. The odds of my not getting a dose of this down the line are minimal.) I was in a depressed, modestly paranoid stupor. I still hung out in the frat house that had both coddled me and stunted my emotional growth. When I overheard a frat brother on the phone planning a bike trip across Europe, I thought I had found an escape route to happiness. He was talking about going to Denmark, Germany, and France.

I pictured myself surrounded by girls at Oktoberfest. I

thought I could handle the cycling. I was in decent shape, despite the fact that, as the great Rodney Dangerfield once said, "My whole body was bloodshot." I still played hoops once a week and ran a lot. Hearing about the bike trip, I was attracted to the excitement in my buddy's voice, something I had long lost. I guess I thought, *Hey, I'm a mess, I can't go out and get a job right now, so why not go along with these guys on their trip?*

So I paid one hundred dollars for a bike on the day of the trip. I met up with the guys at the airport and almost instantly they picked up on my apathy. I was completely uninterested in their maps and routing discussions and only concerned with getting a good gin and tonic on the plane.

These were serious cyclists. Their conversations revolved around agendas, times, equipment, and food supplements. I was just consumed with filling the vast void inside of me. I was glib and void of charm. Sullen and unfocused, I had nothing to contribute.

Anal, nerdy, and resourceful, the guys on the trip had the best equipment and gadgets. If someone wondered what the temperature was, another happy cyclist would dig into his bag and produce a thermometer. They had grip tape, sewing kits, tweezers, ratchet sets, Sterno stoves, hand warmers, foul weather gear, flares, lighters, extra matches stored in a plastic bag, stamps, various lotions, razors, pumps, can openers, computer games, a camp popcorn popper (a little gay), lots of trail mix, Spam, assorted canned goods, and dried fruit. All I had in my cheap book bag were a couple pairs of socks and a *How to Do France* book my mother had given me. As far as clothing, I had what I was wearing: biking shorts and a Coors T-shirt. Incidentally, I was at least twenty pounds overweight and smoked heavily. If my aloofness had not already contaminated the trip's momentum on the plane, I immediately dragged the group down once we landed.

The shit really hit the fan when we landed in London. My cheap bike gave me problems right off the bat. In order to load my bike on the plane in New York, I had to remove the back wheel, a simple procedure that I had been unable to handle. So I manipulated a frat brother, another Jeff, into doing it for me. While Jeff was happy to help me out in New York, he was less enthusiastic about helping me once we landed, for the simple fact that he had to put his own bike back together. As I tried to put the wheel on myself, I revealed to my fellow travelers my inability to work with my hands (opening a can of tuna fish can be challenging for me) and my unwillingness to try. I am not, however, afraid to ask people for help, something I am rather good at.

After I delayed the group for a half hour, we were finally off. At first it was fun. We had not gone even five miles, but I was sure I could keep up with these cyclists. In fact, they were moving so slowly I thought that maybe I should take the lead. I was in Europe! This was a new beginning. Perhaps, I had finally found my calling: to be a leader.

Two hours later I had a rash and a blister, and the car fumes from the crowded highway were making me feel nauseated. In those two hours, my bike had broken down twice. Both times I had to wait for Jeff to come back and fix it for me. A decent soul, Jeff had the patience of a saint. The problem was that the spokes kept breaking. Jeff patiently tried to show me how to fix the problem myself.

I attempted to placate him by looking as focused as possible, nodding my head as I pretended to listen to him. (When someone explains something technical to me, I usually go into a dreamlike state, my eyes glazing over and all.) We had twenty-five miles to go to reach our first camp, which was somewhere on the outskirts of London. While panting and in serious pain, I had a good endorphin rush going and was sure I could make it.

When we pulled into camp hours later, my euphoria was gone, swept away by the relentless car fumes and the blister on my heel. The most important thing was that I had made it to the destination. The camp was not the Ritz, but it would do. As Jeff was informing me about various ointments that would help my blister and rash, I tuned him out again, distracted by the smell of food that the others were preparing on a Sterno stove.

As always, I volunteered to clean up knowing that I would manage to avoid it when the time came. Until recently, I have never "cleaned up" in my entire life. On the trip I went through the obligatory motions like bringing dishes to the sink, but my efforts were cosmetic, anemic, and for the most part un-substantial. I thought I would make up for it by buying them beers later or by picking up the tab at a nice restaurant using the "emergency-use-only" credit card my parents had given me. But scrape hardened noodles from a metal pot? No way. After dinner, I got my hands on a box of chocolates, justifying the gluttonous act as a reward for my thirty-five miles of bicycling. To the chagrin of the others, I devoured the entire box. In a daze, bordering on a diabetic state, I drifted off to sleep without showering or brushing my teeth.

The next morning at six, I awoke to the sound of rain beating down on the small tent, which I had had no role in assembling. *Great*, I thought. Due to the inclement weather, we would postpone our departure time of seven and sleep in a bit. Perhaps we would have brunch at some four-star hotel. Maybe take in a historic castle or two. Then spend the rest of the day at a pub. After all, I had a credit card.

As I entertained these pleasant thoughts, I heard voices outside yelling over the rain. I poked my head out of the tent and looked out incredulously. There they were, decked out in their state-of-the-art rain gear and hunched over a small stove preparing oatmeal. *This is not how Europe should be done*, I thought as I reluctantly stuffed my sleeping bag back into its sack, probably the only chore I could do myself. I should have realized that I was very, very different from the men outside. They were athletes and in great shape. I was not. They were inspired to absorb as much European culture as possible. I simply wanted to absorb as much beer and foreign pussy as humanly possible. (Not so much the latter, actually. I think that all the drugs I had done had weakened my libido. That and the lashing my balls took from those goddamn bike seats. There were no seats built to protect one's prostate back in 1988. It is no wonder my orgasms today have the consistency of skim milk.)

I should have aborted the trip right there and used my parents' credit card to buy a train pass. I'm sure that eventually I would have met up with people more of my temperament, with whom I could have ingratiated myself and from whom I could have possibly bought some blow. Unfortunately, I was not a dynamic thinker or problem solver. In spite of my expensive liberal arts education, I had no critical thinking skills.

I gathered my stuff, mounted my uncooperative bike, and took my place in line to battle the elements and conquer Europe. We had to be in Amsterdam by noon. That was not so easy, though. Through the wind and rain I pedaled on, attempting to shield myself behind the others. However, they were too strong. My spoke problem began to occur every hour or so, and poor Jeff had to keep coming back to help me. I felt like a jerk. After a while, I finally told him to go on ahead without me. He had no problem with that, nor did the others. I had mixed feelings about letting the group go. Sure, the riding was a wholesome activity, but I simply was not prepared for it.

Thank God, I had the credit card. I was emancipated. In Amsterdam, I immediately went to the Heineken Brewery for the brewery tour, where I proceeded to get shit-faced on free samples. That night I wandered around Amsterdam eating, drinking, and smoking hash. I am surprised I did not get a prostitute in the red light district. Or did I?

The next morning, I went to a travel agent to buy my Eurail pass, which cost about two hundred American dollars. I handed my parents' credit card to the man behind the counter, and with one quick and careless gesture my European trip took a major turn for the worse. As the agent ran the card through one of those huge devices they used to have, it seemed to catch. The man tried again, forcing it. It cracked. The card had broken in two.

"No good," he said, handing the card back indifferently. For whatever reason, I could not find a bank in Amsterdam that could help me. I tried to call my parents in New York, but they were away traveling. I was broke and had a broken emergency credit card. Several phone calls to the VISA people proved ineffective.

The following week was hideous. I was relegated to biking all day, sleeping in the woods, and stealing bread from local stores—certainly not the way I had expected to "do Europe."

The worst time was riding my damaged bike through Germany. I actually started to sob like a lost and lonely child. Meanwhile, everyone else seemed to be having fun. With my chafed thighs and filthy clothes, I pushed my bike by crowded outdoor cafés as my contemporaries drank chardonnay. (To this day when I see people laughing and having fun at a sidewalk café I feel like protesting loudly "No fair. You all have plenty of dopamine and brain cells!")

I will admit that at this time I had begun to clap again, a disturbing impulse that managed to stay dormant through the college years. (Praise the Lord!) I would sit on a park bench, my mind racing, when out of the blue I would do three quick claps to the alarm of nearby pedestrians.

However, there was little time to daydream. I had to be in Switzerland in two weeks because that was where I was departing from. Luckily, Europe is a small continent. You can travel from one country to another on a bike in a day. Still, in order to expedite matters, I snuck onto trains, and a couple of times I was thrown off. There were other stressful incidents. An irate apple farmer chased me after he witnessed me poaching one of his apples. Another time, while hitchhiking, a German couple was having a vicious argument and began driving very, very fast. I was sure I was on a death ride. I was certain they would send us careening over the side of the mountain. The guy then turned his fury on me.

"The problem with you Americans—blah, blah, blah, blah!" he roared.

When I finally arrived in Switzerland, I had a few days to kill. Taken with the magnificent snowcapped Alps, I snuck onto what I thought was a local train out to the mountains. I pictured myself high up in the Alps singing, devoid of inhibition, like Heidi. However, the train was not going to the mountains. I ended up in Milan, Italy. Unlike Amtrak, European trains make very few stops, and I was forced to ride a train for another day back to my original spot.

I finally did climb a mountain, sort of. It took me three hours of traipsing through thick brush just to get to the base. The base consisted of mostly gravel, and as I tried to ascend, I made it up one hundred feet only to slide back down in an avalanche of gravel and rock. I tried several times, then aborted my attempt to conquer the Alps.

Adding salt to my wounds, at the first place I tried to sleep I was assaulted by angry, hostile, and vicious ants. When I relocated, I fell asleep again sobbing. Ironically, I woke up feeling refreshed and independent.

AND SO TO WORK: NICHOLS ENTERPRISES

Upon my return to New York City I knew that I was not prepared for the corporate world. I was living fifty miles north of NYC at my parents' large summer house.

I decided to reactivate a company that once thrived when I was in my teens: Nichols Enterprises. Back then I would simply do odd jobs: clean gutters, water plants, weed gardens, et cetera. Now, I figured I would assemble some of my burnout friends, broaden the scope a bit, and try my hand at house painting.

My stepbrother Mike helped me land my first job. One day I was working on the back of a house when my ADD reared its ugly head. My stepbrother rounded the corner and observed the mess I had made. Trees, plants, and screens were liberally splattered with white paint. After surveying the damage, rather than reacting with appropriate indignation and rage, he took a craftier, more effective path.

"Jeff, when you paint, do you let your mind wander? You know, do you think about a lot of different stuff? And maybe fantasize a bit?" he queried pleasantly.

"Yes, yes I do!" I replied happily. Sensing identification, I had taken the bait.

"Well, don't!" he bellowed, *"Focus on painting the motherfucking house!"* I had led with the proverbial chin on this one, and he had given me the knockout punch.

Though it should have, this incident did not deter me in the least. Nichols Enterprises had to go on. To this day I still cannot enter certain counties in upstate New York due to lawsuits.

Once, while painting a wealthy type-A businessman's house in Westchester, I almost lost my life. Mr. Dyer worked at home and was a nice enough guy. He expressly instructed me not to bother him when he was in his office, no matter what happened. This particular house was perched on a cliff overlooking a lake. The job was not going well (spilt paint, over budget, yada yada). I was trying to hit a spot on the highest eave of the house without a ladder because roof shingles provide remarkable footing, anchoring a person like grip tape on a skateboard.

So I was on the ledge and had a shot at the eave if I stood on my toes, but I did not know what to do with the full paint can. I managed to hang it off a shutter, precariously at best. As I moved to paint the spot, I knocked over the bucket, sending the paint everywhere. Within seconds, what were once my stable "grip tape" shingles had now turned into a virtual ice rink. I had no footing at all. I reached out in desperation for anything to avoid a free fall to certain disaster. I managed to lodge two fingers into the hinges of an Andersen window.

Now, feet dangling in air, fat body covered in paint, thrashing, fingers shaky and bleeding, I was actually forced to decide what would be more pleasant: to call out Mr. Dyer, the man who told me in no uncertain terms that if the world exploded not to interrupt him, or to take the hundred-foot fall. (Which considering the depression I was in at the time was not without its appeal.)

I opted to call out, to shriek for life. Mr. Dyer's office was over the garage but close enough to hear and see me.

"What is it?" he yelled.

"Call 911!" I screamed.

When he looked out and saw my predicament, he acted quickly. Thank God, for as soon as my trembling fingers gave way, I started to slide as if I were on some ride at an action park, albeit a ride I would not be able to buy another ticket for ever again.

There was paint all over the roof, and I was completely covered with paint as well. I slid and was about to catapult over the edge of the house when I noticed a ladder. I was not near it, but it gave me some hope. Nearing the edge, I was able to slow myself up just enough to grab onto the gutter. At this point Mr. Dyer was able to negotiate the ladder underneath me. I slowly descended the ladder. I cannot recall if I was crying, but we were both certainly shaken up.

My "distorted sense of entitlement" was fully activated during my time running Nichols Enterprises. Most of my clients were home owners who lived in the city and came out only on the weekends. Trusting souls, they often gave me the keys to their homes. I would often raid the refrigerators and then nod off in front of the television. Of course, I was always on the clock.

THE MAN

After I ran Nichols Enterprises into the ground, it was time to hit Manhattan and join the Establishment. Manhattan had its appeal because I could drink as much as I wanted and not have to worry about driving. The problem was that I had a huge ego and no real job skills.

What I did have going for me in abundance were good connections. One of my parents' friends got me a job as a sales assistant at Merrill Lynch. Granted, it was not a position in the company's coveted training program, but I was assured that it was the best way to learn the business. Because it entailed only administrative work, I was a glorified secretary for three stockbrokers (real animals).

It was the worst possible job for a screwed-up dyslexic like myself. I was eventually fired, and I recall what a scene I caused when I was let go. I thought I was The Man. I could chug beer; I was a people person; and people liked me, goddamnit. People really liked me! I really believed that I was destined for greatness and that I would take any company that was lucky enough to have me to new heights of productivity.

"Do you know who I am?" I indignantly lashed back at the boss who fired me.

"Yes. Yes, I know exactly who you are. You have some sort of learning problem. You have broken three photocopy machines. Complaints come in that you are weird, you are incompetent, and often stink of booze," he replied, not hesitating for a second.

"I will show you!" I walked out in a rage.

Still wanting to be the next Gordon Gecko, I went to work on the floor of the New York Mercantile Exchange (immortal-

74

ized in such movies as *Trading Places* with Eddie Murphy). The commodities traded were things like orange juice, cotton, and gold. I worked in the oil pit with the operations department. At first glance, it was an exciting and vibrant place—the whole building had orange carpeting.

Operations was by far the lowest of the low in the hierarchy of the male-dominated world at the Mercantile Exchange. The top guys were up in an office somewhere calling the shots. Next were the traders, who could only be described as pit bulls in suits. In fact, the only things that separated these guys from the guys placing bets at the local OTB were the suits and the fact that they didn't smell of urine. Very few of these "businessmen" had college degrees. Below them were the runners who ran the orders back and forth and were aspiring traders. Below them were operations. What happens at the "Merc" is that a pack of guys sit around something called the "pit," which was exactly what it was—a hole in the ground with rims almost like the Greek Coliseum seating where the brokers stood. The entire place was bright yellow.

From what I can remember, all the brokers did was scream numbers and dates at each other in a hysterical manner.

"OCT AT EIGHTY!"

"OCT AT EIGHTY-FIVE!"

What they were doing, as I understand it, was not trading oil but hedging on what the oil price would be at a future date. When they found a buyer, they would scribble the order down on a piece of paper and throw it into the pit where some poor bastard would gather them all up and put them in a chute—like what they have at a bank drive-through—to be registered. That poor bastard, eventually, would be me.

My first job was to sit next to a trader and whenever he made a trade, I would translate the trade via hand signals to a guy on a podium. No job could amplify a person's dyslexia like this. Actually, it could be the definitive diagnostic test.

The broker would scream out the numbers and I would have to both remember them and regurgitate them in order via hand signals—a dyslexic's nightmare. After a week of fucking up just about every order, I was relegated to the worst job possible: the "pit guy" who collected the cards with the orders scribbled on them.

Only a picture, or a better wordsmith than I, could capture how ridiculous was the job of the "gatherer." I had to wear *goggles* because these often coked-up animals would whip the order cards at such a high velocity that they easily could cut one's retina. Once I actually had a card imbedded in my forehead.

To make matters worse, I was ensconced in a huge net. It draped around my neck, and like an octopus gathering food, I would retrieve the cards. Only my hands and head appeared through the net.

God, I looked moronic. I wanted to give them the benefit of the doubt, but I truly believe the guys purposely tried to hit my forehead with the sharp order cards. There was nothing I could do anyway, stoned all the time. (For that job, who could really blame me?) I think that even if I tried to attack my tormentors, I would have inevitably gotten snarled in the huge net and rolled around in it like some kind of animal being captured in the wild. The more I would have struggled, the more ensnarled I would have gotten, probably to the delight of onlookers.

I was still going to bars to get my "sway on," but it was not working anymore. The booze had lost its magic. My main watering hole was Dorrian's Red Hand, home of the Preppie murder scandal with Robert Chambers. I did not know him, but I knew both the bar proprietors, the Dorrian brothers, Michael and John. John actually went to grammar school with me at a place called The Day Schools (now called Trevor Day). He was a good friend to me, a nice genuine guy. I remember hanging around the restaurant as a kid and riding in his grandfather's station wagon—he apparently was a legend in the restaurant business—down to the meat packing district. The family was always nice to me . . . but toward the end of my drinking, even they had had enough.

There were some ridiculous and humiliating incidents toward the end of my drinking. One time, when living with my parents on Park Avenue, I came home in the midst of a blackout and apparently could not get the key in the lock. Instead I opted to roll myself up in the door mat in the hallway and go to sleep, which is where I woke up the next morning. With horror I realized that, at eleven a.m., every tenant including my parents, all showered and freshly groomed, had to step over me on their way to work. It was time for AA.

SOBRIETY SUCKS

I do believe if there is truly a disease called alcoholism, I probably have it. The reason being, when my girlfriend talks about winning the lottery, she imagines buying a new house. When I think about a lotto windfall, I picture a six-month coke and hooker run in Las Vegas.

AA saved my life. No question. But, really, I went to AA for four reasons (not in order): 1) to obtain some identification, fellowship, and solace; 2) to meet women (or at least be exposed to women); 3) to work on my comedy material; 4) to hand out flyers for my comedy show to unsuspecting newcomers.

Although AA is obviously an anonymous program, it is a large part of my story and after much deliberation I feel it is all right to mention it. I believe that AA, at its best, and all twelve-step programs, for that matter, are wonderful and divinely inspired. For sure, there are a lot of good people affecting positive change in those rooms. As a rule, AA does not like it when high-profile people talk about the program. It would rather use attraction than promotion to help others. Seeing that I am far from famous, unless you consider a couple appearances on NY1 and the Luggage Channel to be high-profile, I feel that I can talk some about my experience.

Also I suppose I am a bit irreverent or a revisionist, but I believe some adjustments should be made to AA's archaic steps and traditions. For one, caffeine, a narcotic by any standard, and cigarettes should be discouraged as unsober behavior. They are not. Also, I think that just as the Catholic Church should have addressed the issue of homosexuality and child abuse, AA should admit publicly that it has a problem with fraternization. Or more crudely put: affairs are often spurred on in the rooms of AA. Biology being what it is, put men and women in a room together and that's what happens. Anyone who says that inappropriate love affairs do not occur in AA quite simply has his head up his ass. AA destroys more marriages than booze.

While I am at it, AA was conceived for people with problems with alcohol, but these days it seems to have evolved into a program that caters to the drug addict as much as the alcoholic. This operates on the theory that a "drug is a drug," but I do not think this is the case. I believe a drug addict has a more calculating disposition than your garden-variety drunk. One time I was sitting next to a heroin addict who used to sell guns and rob houses in East Hampton. He asked me for my phone number. That's what you do in AA—give out your phone number to strange heroin addicts. I gave it to him, but leaving the meeting I was asking myself, *What the fuck did I do that for? That man should be in jail.* Also I am not sure if I believe in the "disease theory" in regards to these conditions. I might be a simpleton or cold-hearted, but I think anyone who is ruining their lives with drugs and alcohol should quite simply *stop* drinking and drugging, or as they say in AA, put the "plug in the jug."

My first meeting was on the Upper East Side of Manhattan. I went with a friend from college who was also ready for the Hobart party to end. I expected to see a bunch of down-and-out Blarney Stoned drunks there. Instead, there were about one hundred well-dressed professional types.

"You know, I really would never have suspected those people of being alcoholics, perhaps guilty of a little insider trading, but not alcoholism," my friend remarked as we left.

So began my incredible sixteen-year run in AA. Some people refer to it as the "best show in town for a dollar." Because people are being honest, truly speaking from the heart, the stories can be absolutely hilarious, not to mention shocking. (Let me add that if you go to an AA meeting without a genuine desire to stop drinking, a bolt of lightning should strike you down.) At its best, AA is a sacred place where people get better physically, mentally, and spiritually. At its worst, AA is a catty lot of gossipers and opportunists. Regardless, it is a place that people can use as a sober reference point and to have their feelings validated.

As I understand it, the Native Americans used to sit around in a circle and pass around a talking stick. Whoever had the stick had the floor, so to speak. AA meetings work in the same fashion. It is about dialogue and connecting with other people who have a desire to stop drinking. It is also about what it is like to live a spiritual life helping others, free from the confines of one's own ego. How can that be bad?

Twelve-step programs are unaccommodating to the learning disabled. There. I said that, too. This may seem trivial, but consider this: Aside from verbal dialogue, AA is all about books and writing. A newcomer is inundated with pamphlets and other supplementary reading materials when leaving a meeting. Either you are reading a "step" in the "Big Book," the cornerstone of the program and a five-hundred-page anachronism, or you are writing about your experience with whatever step you are working on.

At the second meeting I went to, a woman pleasantly handed me the AA preamble—which is only five lines—to read in front of the group. I orally butchered it and never returned to that meeting again. AA has several types of meetings. At "Big Book" meetings everyone in the group reads a paragraph aloud. I wonder how many people burdened with learning disabilities would opt for a public enema over reading aloud.

The steps are in a certain order for a reason, and it is suggested that participants follow this order. As I have established, learning-disabled people hate order and tend to rebel against it instinctively. Some of the steps are downright academic. I wanted to do a fourth step with my sponsor (take a thorough and fearless moral inventory of myself), and he presented me with what was essentially an economic flowchart. I had to put things in columns and boxes. I can see how academic people thrive in twelve-step programs.

Although I hate to read publicly, I began to get addicted to speaking publicly. For a grandiose opportunist like myself, AA can become a nifty little public speaking venue. As a professional comedian, I would often go for the laugh rather than honesty and growth. I began to chase the laughs with the same vigor and enthusiasm that I used to chase drugs and alcohol.

Many times my interest was transparent. At one meeting everyone was getting laughs. The speaker was honest, relaxed, and therefore funny. Her energy was contagious and everyone who shared after her was funny as well. I was salivating in the back of the room with my hand up, desperately hoping to be called on. After all, I was a professional comedian, and these people were amateurs. I could take the room to new heights of laughter. Although I occasionally stuttered, it was the risk I took for the high from getting laughs. Getting laughs is as good as scoring goals in a lacrosse game. With laughs comes a certain amount of bliss, power, and omnipotence. Like a drug, you start to chase it and stay in constant pursuit of it.

I was finally called on, and I suppose I came across as artificial, a bit too contrived for the crowd. I was forcing the laughs, and the captive audience did not give it up for me. When I did not receive the expected and desired laugh from my first little bit, panic struck. I desperately tried old stuff that I knew was funny, for I had used it before. Stuff about having too much coffee at a meditation meeting got only silence from the audience: "Sit back, relax, and let your mind race." I recall my friend who sat next to me cringing in embarrassment. The masochistic part is that I babbled on for about five minutes despite realizing that my humor was not working. Pathetically, I tried to switch gears and go for the empathy. How I was suffering from an "incurable disease" and all. It was awful.

Not only did I bomb at an AA meeting full of newcomers who needed help, but I also contaminated the place with negative energy. I must have set off a bad vibe because no one came up to me after the meeting except one guy who pulled me aside and told me that before I tried my act at Madison Square Garden, I should try out some smaller venues in the Bronx and Queens.

I was never asked to qualify (tell my story) in meetings. There is a speaking circuit in the New York AA. I am always amazed at how articulate, insightful, and funny the speakers are. The lion's share of my AA experience has been in Manhattan, though I have been to meetings all over the country. In other places, it seems, meetings are designed to help the real drunkard. In Manhattan, God forbid a real street drunk shows up. He will clear the room like Michael Jackson showing up at a day-care center.

I wish I was joking here or even exaggerating, but I am not. People with real alcohol problems fuck up the meeting. Who wants a smelly drunk around when you are trying to sound good and meet chicks? Again, please keep in mind that my experience is with Upper East Side, New York City, AA meetings. But, I believe that there is an opinion in AA today that alcoholics should go to rehab first, then AA. Well this may seem nice in theory, but with state and national budget cuts and insurance companies no longer green-lighting long-term rehab stays, AA better get back to its primary purpose of helping drunks sober up. Because they are coming your way.

By the way, nothing magnifies the Manhattan AA social hierarchy more than the holiday season. Like any human organization, AA has cliques, but the velvet ropes come out during the Christmas party season. And breaking into the A-list Manhattan sober holiday party circuit is no easy feat. Brian, a charismatic art broker, was famous for large sober soirees to which only the blueblood WASP or the supercool Jew was invited. People would actually cruise meetings to find Brian and try to land an invite. But Brian did not get as far as he did in the AA scene by being reckless with his invite list. Brian made no mistakes: no trust fund, no invite. I remember how left out I felt when I was not invited. Looking back, I realize it was all so ridiculous. Sober Christmas parties suck ass. No one has fun at sober parties. Gone are the merriment and the possibility of getting a drunken hand job in the broom closet. There's no booze, and everyone eats too many cookies and drinks too many Diet Cokes. By midnight, the guests leave gassy.

I'm not sure if it was my so-called Tourette's, but I did on some rare occasions clap during the meetings and also let out some loud groans. I was also clearly in the throes of massive caffeine addiction. I could not sit still and always came across disheveled (Chronic Slob). Funny, but if you are an accomplished artist and you come across disheveled, you are considered a creative eccentric. However, if not successful and disheveled, you are treated like a mental patient. On the rare occasion that I was asked to speak I was always too candid. I would talk about how full of lust I was and how I thought I deserved to get laid. And how the AA principles were a form of communism.

I cannot say that the only reason I went to AA was to hear myself talk or to meet women (which happened twice in twelve years), but those are certainly incentives for going. Plus, I did not want to go to bars. Where the hell else was I supposed to go? Yoga and cooking classes intimidated the hell out of me.

One positive feature that AA offers that seems to be effective at keeping people from drinking is something called the "service commitment." A newcomer would sign up to set up at the meeting, stack chairs at the end of the meeting, or make coffee once a week. Not wanting to disappoint the group, he or she would not drink all week so he or she could do his or her service commitment. People do not want to let down their new peer group. This does work. Still, I am convinced that the majority of people in AA would not show up if there was not the remote possibility for sex, job opportunities, improved social status, and networking. I went there because I was fucking lonely. That's okay. But I did not go there to help a strung out cokehead gather bus fare to get back to Virginia—God forbid I had to deal with a *real* drunk there. I guess that makes me a dick.

A learning disability is not a reason to not do the steps. It is just that I had to work through my fear of the structure. And for that I needed a good sponsor. Finding one, in my opinion, is as tough as finding a good shrink, which is nearly impossible, but I did find one.

A NARCOTIC BY ANY STANDARD

Another fundamental problem I had, and still have with AA, is that I am a massive caffeine addict. Three or four huge cups of coffee a day. Plus a Diet Coke (20 ounces during the afternoon). Why is this bad? One of the fundamental tenets of AA is prayer and meditation. In order to build the necessary relationship to a higher power you must open yourself up and work on the connection. Being a caffeine addict, I can honestly and seriously tell you that if someone gave me a choice between a constant contact with a benevolent higher power and a huge industrial-size vat of Dunkin' Donuts coffee, I would opt for the coffee.

Anyway, they say it is progress, not perfection. One time I went to a meditation meeting in Central Park, and before it began we all sat around and sucked off a giant urn of coffee. To me it is impossible to meditate while on coffee: sit back . . . relax . . . and . . . *let your mind race!*

It is important to emphasize that AA helped me in many ways.

However, I wonder how real celebrities, people in the arts or sciences who are not bottom feeders like me, manage to fare in AA, because one of the AA messages is about ego deflation. "You are not unique" is stressed often. Being a "worker among workers" and becoming a "choir member" are fundamental principles of AA. Thinking about it, one could almost say it is downright socialism, which is great for people like me who are unrealistically grandiose and remarkably self-centered to the point of hurting others.

If I were a real genius, however, I would take issue with these tenets of AA. Sure, I want to stop drinking, but if it's not about me, who the fuck is it about? Humility, after all, is simply honest self-appraisal. When Muhammad Ali claimed he was the greatest, he was humble, for he was indeed the greatest. Okay, ego can be overdone certainly, but at the end of the day a certain amount of it is good and should be celebrated, not discouraged.

I used to have a sponsor, Eddie, who was good-natured, albeit a bit of a simpleton. (Not that simple is necessarily bad. See the movie *Being There* with Peter Sellers as a simple person who made his way up from gardener to millionaire.) I am not sure if it was because of AA or not, but Eddie really got into the principles and the tenets of the program.

I would see Eddie every day at the end of a meeting, and he would ask me how was my day. I would then, in scatological jittery fashion, tell him my day's events: I just got out of jail for jumping a subway turnstile, stole silverware from my grandmother, and have been regularly fantasizing about having sex with a twelve-year-old Korean boy. At this Eddie would look at me, puzzled, as if trying to absorb it all. (I was certainly a tough case.) Finally, he would ask me if I had drunk that day. I told him honestly that I had not.

"Then you're a winner today!" he would say with confidence,

suddenly getting his focus back. No longer was he confused, for he managed to summon a nice AA slogan from his reservoir. The fact that I did not drink apparently neutralized all of the immoralities and wiped the slate clean.

Eddie was really into helping newcomers to AA. He felt, as AA does in general, that if one does not help another person from staying away from a drink, then the Samaritan himself will eventually drink. He demanded that I approach at least three newcomers every meeting and give them my number. I approached newcomers reluctantly because I did not feel like I would be doing them any favors, quite frankly. I did not even have a business card.

One guy called me for help. He was obviously strung out from a long run on crack. (Look up the word *mess* in a dictionary and you will see a picture of this guy.) We went out for dinner after a meeting (AA protocol). Halfway into the meal, this guy, this crack addict, started to console me. Telling me not to worry and that things would be okay. He even offered me money, which I reluctantly took. (Look, things were bad.) When he left me, I was sobbing. That was basically the extent of my newcomer experience.

While I love AA, it certainly gets a tad boring being sober. I heard someone mention in a meeting that AA was a "church mouse existence." For ten years I attended a meeting on Friday nights with a friend of mine. Year after year we would leave the meeting and participate in what we later dubbed affectionately the "walk of shame." We would walk down Second Avenue through a gauntlet of bars packed with people having fun and, of course, drinking. Not wanting to drink ourselves (because somehow we had lost the privilege of solace along the way), we kept our heads down and walked all the way down to our apartment on the Lower East Side.

One Friday night we were watching a Knicks game, and I remember I thought it was cold, so I draped a blanket over me like a shawl, then covered my feet with another blanket. We were both eating ice cream, and somehow the discussion turned to what kind of sherbet we were partial to. I preferred orange creamscicle, while he opted for raspberry. Then it occurred to us, almost simultaneously, that we, draped in blankets, were having the type of conversation that probably one hundred people in the same complex over the age of seventy were having. Thank God, we eventually found "fun in sobriety"—biking, skiing, and going to concerts. If an alcoholic does not do this stuff, the sherbet might turn into a beer one night.

Unable to go to bars, I was restricted to high-end coffee shops. Places like DT UT on the East Side of Manhattan had warm, inviting atmospheres, but one look at the crowd and it is clear why velvet ropes and guest lists exist. There were some cool folk among the randoms. My problem was that I was so used to relying on booze as my social lubricant that it was tough to get my groove on after guzzling six espressos and inhaling a lemon tart.

When I tried to approach girls, I would sweat and stutter like a madman. I must have looked like a combination of Rain Man and Forrest Gump on crack. Suffice it to say, the group of women first ignored me, then they vaporized.

God forbid I stare at a woman in AA, even though some women come in with outrageous stories about how they banged every guy in the Western Hemisphere while wasted. Of course, biology being what it is, I stare at them, jaw open. Then, of course, I get labeled as a pervert. Hey, if the ladies do not want me to stare at them, they should go a little lighter on the blowing-guys-in-bathrooms stories. You are supposed to share in a "general way."

If AA becomes a guy's sole place to meet women, which it was for me, that guy should get ready to die on the vine. This is not to say that people do not often hook up at meetings, for they certainly do. But the stars have to align just so. To my knowledge, you cannot simply approach a girl at AA in the same way you would at a bar or party without getting blasted in the face with Mace and kicked in the balls by her or her protective sponsor. Before you make your move you have to be accepted by the group and be considered funny and bright. Only then can you bang your brains out. The point is, if you go to AA meetings with the sole purpose of meeting women, you will probably be disappointed, spiritually enlightened perhaps but pussy-less nonetheless, just as I was.

The worst time I ever had in AA was at a sober dance. Good God, did I feel like less than. I sat on the periphery of the gyrating multitudes and fought back feelings of utter inadequacy—the exact type of feeling that made me want to crawl into a bottle of Jack Daniel's when I was in middle school. Now I know: if you happen to attend one of these events, grab someone. Anyone. Dance your rear off, it is your only salvation. You must participate!

Sobriety is tough. Finding serenity is even tougher. Not being able to change your mood via substances is almost unnatural; all beings should be entitled to some sort of solace. Some shelter from the storm. I read somewhere that some species of fish occasionally bang their heads against a rock to alter their mood. To be able to cut loose is important. The goal in AA is to find ways of escape that do not end in a six-month prison stay. Spirituality, if achieved, has to be better than banging one's head against a rock.

Unfortunately, I am not a very good AA member. I am not that guy who used to be a horrific drug addict shooting heroin in the bathrooms of municipal parks and who with divine intervention became a sober, responsible being whose primary purpose in life is to serve and help others. I believe disposition is innate to a person. AA is not going to make a bad person good. I don't believe that I am necessarily a bad person, but I have never understood the socialist tendencies (and slogans) of AA. "We are not unique," "We are choir members," or—and I hated this one more than anything else—"I am no better or worse than anyone else." Fuck anyone who professes that statement. I can almost guarantee that he does not believe it. And, if someone really does believe it, he is wrong.

I am better than some people (though not many). I firmly believe there must be some motherfucker out there who I am "better" than. Sure, I have not found him/her yet, but when I do, we both will know it.

Although technically "sober," I have become a massive caffeine, sugar, and nicotine addict. I use these drugs to fill the empty hole inside me. The hole that shouts out that I am just an average guy or, even more unthinkable, below average. The hole that suspects that I am not a big shot after all.

Coffee allows me to stay in a pleasant state of delusion. I have replaced booze with coffee and sugar, and I am not sure which one is better, to be honest. You might argue that you will not crash a car on too much coffee or sugar. To this I ask, How do you know that? I doubt that the person who commits "road rage" is sucking on an herbal tea. I have seen a fair number of sober people in AA lose legs due to diabetes because they did not respect the power of sugar.

At my most cynical times I find people who bash alcohol and their drinking days to be ingrates. Who are these people to marginalize the thousands of years of solace and escape that alcohol has provided to civilization? Did Benjamin Franklin not say that "Beer is proof that God loves us and wants us to be happy"? For many people alcohol acts as a marvelous social lubricant and, bluntly put, it got a lot of us laid.

THE NINTH STEP

Eddie was also big on something called the ninth step, where alcoholics make a list of people they have harmed, track them down, and apologize to them. This is more for the sake of "cleaning up one's side of the street" than helping the victim of your filthy, often unforgivable behavior. The ninth step is the most abused step there is!

Eddie prodded me to go out and make amends to a kid I went to boarding school with. Several years earlier I had pretty much ruined his wedding by, among other things, conspicuously making out with his grandmother, doing shots of Sambuca with the bartender until she could not function and was sent home, and trashing a hotel room that had the groom's credit card number for the deposit. I also took a family heirloom (an old life preserver ring with the name of their family ferry-service business and start date) off the wall and ended up running down the street, jumping into the back of a pickup truck, and demanding the driver to drive (he did not) before being brought down by an angry mob of guests in suits.

I went to see the guy, a hardworking decent fellow, and he was a little standoffish. I told him I was an alcoholic and he basically asked me how that would help him get back his wedding night.

So I would say, fuck the ninth step. If you cause this much destruction, the best thing you could do for this guy is send him a hundred grand. Going up to him and saying "Hey, I am sorry I ruined your wedding, I am an alcoholic," means jack shit—you are an asshole. How is reminding him that you were a filthy drunk going to save his wedding?

SOBRIETY: THE COST

Not drinking is a complete wet blanket on a first date. I hate to reduce everything to a formula, but when it comes to making out on a date, no booze = no action. But if both parties have had a few drinks, the chance of a make-out session increases dramatically. Trying to make out with a girl for the first time when there is no booze around is like washing a pan with no soap: it's theoretically possible, but it's not pretty.

I have found that there is no chance a girl will drink if the guy will not. When I tell a girl I do not drink, she automatically feels self-conscious about her drinking (especially if she is a lush). She may order a glass of wine, but she does not polish off the whole bottle when you are drinking a decaf coffee.

I have made out with girls sober a handful of times. In each case it was fun and exciting, but the initial kiss was always abrupt and awkward. Like a trainwreck. Absent is the alcohol that masks the anxiety, neediness, and bad breath.

My worst sober sexual experience was with a cute girl I had met after a New Year's Eve comedy show I did out on Long Island. The girl had actually approached me after the show, which was unusual because my act was incredibly self-deprecating, focusing almost exclusively on my yellow teeth, saggy balls, and premature ejaculation. However, I have noticed that if the guys in the audience like my act, a girl may be interested, no matter how gross I am onstage.

Anyway, this girl was interested, and that night I got her phone number. She was a cute, petite redhead. (I am generally not attracted to redheads, not because they are not pretty but because I find really orange hair to be unsettling and tough on my nervous system.) After a few days, I called her for a date.

It was a snowy day in Manhattan and she came over to the place I was renting from a friend on West Fifty-seventh Street. We rented movies and sat on the couch for hours. Each opportunity I had to make out with her I let slip by. Finally, five coffees later, and with a severe case of dry mouth, I made an awkward, desperate lunge at her just as she was about to go (no doubt wondering what was wrong with me). Surprisingly, she reciprocated. But I was all twitchy from the coffee and the redhead thing had my mind all fucked up. (I have had a problem in the past with a burning sensation in my groin area. In cruder terms, I had burning balls. And I thought that the red vagina might trigger this effect.)

I was pawing away at her when she pushed me back and pulled down her pants a little. When I went to help, she pushed my hand back. She proceeded to play with herself. Every effort I made to get involved and contribute was thwarted.

"Look, if you leave me alone I will come," she finally said. So I sat on the edge of the couch in absolute awe. In hindsight, I probably should have done what she was doing. When she was finished, she pulled her pants up. "I have to go," she said. I spoke to her only once after that.

SOBER SEX: HOOKERS

I fell into a routine over the years. I went to a meeting where I and other New Yorkers would simultaneously romanticize and shun the world of alcohol for an hour. After the meeting, I picked up a pint of Häagen-Dazs and went home to jerk off to *Girls Gone Wild* commercials. The next day I would attend another meeting, hailing the benefits of AA and how, with thanks to AA's principles and a higher power, my life was now "beyond my wildest dreams."

The only break in my routine occurred when I dabbled in the occasional prostitute. Very few of my friends, both in AA and out, will admit that they have used escort services or, as I like to say, "worked the phones." "Working the phones" is picking up a copy of *The Village Voice* and calling a number from the back pages. *The Village Voice*, Manhattan's premiere free paper, was once critically acclaimed but is now used by many as the lust bible and is New York's primary sexual reference point. It consists of ten pages of liberal ramblings, ten pages of music reviews, and sixty pages of ads for sexual services catering to absolutely every fetish in the known world. I counted at least two pages for she-males. Prostitution keeps *The Village Voice* in print.

Nine-tenths of the fun of having a prostitute is the anticipation. What will she look like? What will it be like? Not just anyone can "work the phones." It takes a certain skill, an art if you will. There is a certain language you must use on the phone to ensure a good-looking hooker. For instance, you have to inform them that you are a businessman from out of town who has used their services before and was disappointed. You must state that if she is not good looking, you will not let her in. If you are not assertive on the phone they will send over The

Ugly One. I could say more but I can't give away all the tricks.

My first hooker experiences were pretty straightforward. I would get drunk at Dorian's when I was home from college on break and walk up 85th Street and stagger back to my parents' apartment on East 82nd Street. At the time it was the late eighties and 85th Street between Second and Third had a lot of street walkers on the block. Now when one is twenty years old, drunk, and horny and most of the girls at the bar were not looking at your ugly ass, and some girl on the street comes up to you and says, "Would you like me to suck your dick for ten bucks?" often one's reaction will be "Why, yes. Yes, I would!" And that was the case with me. These women would escort you down below a stairwell and suck on your (often flaccid in my case) cock. Often, while doing it; with your pants around your ankles they would rifle through your pockets and grab your wallet and take off. This happened to my friend who like me was not street savvy. He started to chase her down 85th Street with pants around his ankles, his dick out, screaming, "Stop her! She has my wallet!" I mean, I can't imagine this happening today!

On one occasion I was out at a bar with a college friend of mine, Matt. Matt surveyed the bar scene and our odds of meeting chicks (me with my big nose and he was simply a disaster) and we both decided to go look for professionals early on in the night. Our pockets were stuffed with Christmas money, so we got in a cab and gave the driver $40 as a down payment and said that if he found us a hooker we would give him another $50 or so. About a half hour later, a girl (I hope) got in our car, and instantly both of us had our pants down around our ankles. (Today, looking back, it is such a gross visual I almost feel like vomiting). The girl blew Matt, and the sound effects were so disgusting, it did not work for me. The girl got out of the cab and made off into the night. By the time we pulled our pants up and realized she had stolen all of our money (but kindly left our wallets), she was gone. We started screaming to the cabby, "Find that chick!" By this point, the cab driver was completely disgusted by us. He drove us home. We took his address and promised to send him money. I am sure I lost the address.

I have been with probably ten hookers in my life. I am not proud. One thing for sure is that the despair, remorse, and shame one feels after the deed is done is just as bad as a cocaine depression, if not worse. The remorse is tangible. You feel like the colossal loser that you are. (The worst are the Asian jerk-off places in the city. By the way, they are everywhere. You can stand in any neighborhood in New York and there will be an Asian massage parlor probably within three blocks of you. Any guy who says he has not been to one is probably fibbing.) There is nothing worse than cumming on your stomach and then have an indignant woman throw you a towel while yelling "Next!" One time a girl left her umbrella in my five-story walk-up. I remember opening the umbrella and letting it glide down to her on the street. It worked perfectly. Most times I would get a massage and a hand job.

The greatest thing that ever happened to AA people is something called Match.com. Hallelujah! Online dating has got to be the greatest invention of the twentieth century (aside from GPS and Viagra). After signing up for this wonderful program, I turned from a guy that had vague hope to meet a girl at an upcoming wedding three long months down the road to a guy who could have a date every weekend if I wanted. The only problem was that I did not have a credit card. So, sadly, I had to put it on Mommy's Visa card. (Desperate for grandkids, she went along with it.) But this meant that I was put in the awful position of having to update my mother/investor on my dating process.

"Hi, Mommy! Yes, I am doing very well on Match.com. In fact, I fingered a forty-five-year-old Hungarian woman last night!"

I am always enamored by profiles on Match, even though I find them a bit redundant. Per Match, most women are "avid hikers" who are "not into playing games." I have a hundred female friends and have never heard that they liked hiking (brunch, yes; hiking, no), but according to Match.com, the Appalachian Trail is crowded with "athletic and toned" go-getters who want to "enjoy everything this wonderful city has to offer."

Match.com raises an interesting question: Why do women always say that they want a guy with a great sense of humor? What about handy? You never hear a girl say that they are looking for a "handyman." I think "handy" should trump "funny" any day. This preference allegedly works in my favor, but I admit it: I am not a real man. I am constantly hiring "men" to fix shit in my apartment or boat, as I sit around and wait to pay them.

I used to be painfully candid on my Match.com profile; I directly addressed my concerns about my weak libido and watery orgasms. As one might expect, I got very little response to my ad. I also said that I lived in Queens. When I took that off, the number of responses increased dramatically.

I caught on pretty quickly that Match.com is unforgiving and has little sense of humor. Girls might laugh at your profile, but they certainly are not going to fuck you or even respond to you. They will just click on the next profile in which an attorney describes his favorite ski lodge in Utah and New Year's Eve at the Copacabana (in Cuba).

So I started to talk about international travel and that I was not altogether opposed to the possibilities of tango lessons. I dropped names of expensive restaurants in NYC. I shamelessly played my comic/showbiz card. At last, the game began to pick up. A forty-year-old cannot convince a girl he is "on his way up" like a thirty-year-old can. At forty, either a man is "up" or he'll never finish "his way up." I winked at so many girls on Match and they never winked back. I was always tempted as a joke to send them this note: "Hey, I winked at you, you cunt!"

The problem with internet dating when you don't drink is that once you go out on a date with a girl and she finds out that you are a *nondrinker* the entire date becomes *her* trying to get to the bottom of why *you* are a fucking teetotaler. And if she gets a whiff that you are in AA . . . forget it. That's alarming to women. Red flag! And throwaway lines to impress her, like "When I drank, it was all about the money, the cars, and the women," don't work either. Nor do attempts at humor: "When I drank, I woke up in handcuffs." Once this chick gets a whiff that you're in AA, it's game over. Now if you have other credentials, maybe a large stock portfolio, then she might overlook your history of substance abuse. But when you're a borderline candidate to begin with, you can be sure a second date is not in the cards.

And make no mistake, if you don't drink on a date there will be questions why. To say, "Alcohol just stopped working for me" will not end the questioning. She will want to know specifically to satisfy her curiosity. "What specific incident got you to stop drinking?" she will insist. Finally after trying to play it nice, in a fit of frustration, you will blurt out, "Okay, you really want to know: When I found myself getting a blow job from a tranny behind a Dumpster!" Again, if you were recently seen on the cover of *Forbes* magazine, she might find this story amusing.

Otherwise, you will be faced with the dreaded, "I have to get up early tomorrow morning."

Exit stage right.

YOUNG AND HORNY IN SOBRIETY

Let me say this, and again this is one man's opinion: For your average Joe, trying to date while off the hooch is a nightmare. You are instructed by your support group not to go to bars or parties that serve alcohol. Even if you go to bars, women tend to look at you like you're a complete pussy for not drinking, especially if you refuse a shot. They're thinking: *I mean put down the pom-poms and get in the game!* And you, at the same time, can't help but think to yourself, *What a drunken slut.* You are on two different planes. Thus, as a sober person, one is basically confined to coffee shops, dreary sober dances, horrific sober parties, and brutal sober summer share houses. Why does the sober social scene suck? Simple: because there is no fucking booze! Booze has been around for generations. Throughout time. Why? Simple: it got a whole lot of us laid! Take that marvelous social lubricant away and what do you have? Horny, angry people. I guarantee that most guys that start shooting people in malls are not getting properly laid. Sobriety yes! But at what cost?

They say in the rooms of AA that you should go every day for the rest of your life. Every day? (And it is not just one hour a day, it's more like three, and then there is the fucking meeting after the meeting at the coffee shop.) That bothers me. Do I really want to spend my entire adult life in a plastic folding chair in a church basement? The superintendent of the building that I live in today in New York is a World War II veteran. He is constantly talking about "the War" (the big one) and is full of stories of adventure and travel. What am I going to tell my grandkids, God forbid I have them? "Tell us about your life, Grandpa!"

Me? "Yes, well . . . ah . . . When I was a kid I used to go to *The Rocky Horror Picture Show* on acid and do the time warp dance, and then I went to AA and ate cookies in a church basement for thirty years." Sobriety sucks.

In the end, as bad as sobriety can be, it beats the alternative: dying of cirrhosis of the liver or in a drunk driving accident.

A CURE!!!

At an AA meeting I once butchered a paragraph so completely that a man came up to me afterward and asked me directly if I had a learning disability. When I replied affirmatively, he told me about a doctor in Manhattan who had found a cure for dyslexia.

I told my mother about him and days later I was put on Dr. Emerson's waiting list. I was originally given a date three months away. Apparently a cure for dyslexia draws in the crowds. His rate was a thousand dollars.

I am not sure why I was so desperate to go sooner than my appointed time. I had already made it through thirty-five years of unmitigated chaos. What was another three months? I told the receptionist that I lived very close and could come at any time because I was not working. I got the call that there was an opening and I was off to see Dr. Emerson.

I was simultaneously alarmed, disturbed, saddened, and

amused to find that the waiting room was covered with children's toys. Apparently, like certain cigarette companies, Dr. Emerson targeted a younger demographic.

During the morning an extremely apathetic nurse put me through a bunch of mundane neurological tests that seemed geared around my balance. Stand on one foot. Touch my nose. Walk on a line. Walk foot over foot. Then the nurse spun me around in a chair before blasting a light deep into my retina. During this time she was scribbling stuff down on my chart. She then put me on a computer and asked me to hit the space bar every time I saw a rabbit. This game lasted about an hour and toward the end not only was I still dyslexic but I was also on the brink of utter insanity.

During the course of the test I could not help but think that this was all a bunch of crap, a scam by another opportunistic doctor exploiting children who happen to learn differently. The final test was a hearing test. If you have a learning disability and go looking for medical help, get ready to take a lot of hearing tests. I must have had twenty or thirty electronic hearing tests in my life, all of which I passed.

After about two hours of testing I finally met the doctor. After two minutes I could tell by his jargon that this was a man who had lost all interest in the subject. He appeared to be on autopilot and he never broke out of the "I am talking to an eleven-year-old and his parents" rhythm.

He asked me a lot questions, such as whether I tended to have to go back and read stuff over again. I have to admit that I was a little rude to the guy; all I wanted to talk about was how the drug ecstasy destroyed my brain. His tone started to change to one of a man who was being threatened. For a layman, I knew a fair amount about brain chemistry and asked a lot of specific questions. This ruffled the doctor's feathers.

He told me that I had an inner-ear disturbance and wrote me a prescription for Dramamine. He went on to say that I should wear reading glasses and gave me a quick color test to see what shade of lens would help me. Finally, the doctor told me I should read with a three-by-five card under every line. For a thousand bucks I thought I would get a little more bang for the buck, maybe even, as advertised, a cure for dyslexia.

The only thing my visit to Dr. Emerson got me was a huge dose of self-consciousness. What did he mean by inner-ear malfunction? Did I have a problem with my equilibrium? I tried to get him on the phone, but it seemed as though the doctor was on to the next patient. I consulted a medical encyclopedia at Barnes & Noble, and it said that many inner-ear problems are the result of brain damage.

I staggered out of Barnes & Noble utterly horrified. I had an inner-ear problem! There is something profoundly unsexy/un-athletic about an inner-ear problem. I felt completely defective and remarkably self-conscious. Now I would never get laid.

I was finally beginning to forget about my problems with balance when I was on the subway and saw a guy sporting New Balance sneakers. Ever since that day, I cringe when I see New Balance sneakers. On the basketball court, I have been unable to guard a person wearing that brand of sneaker. I tend to bomb at comedy shows if I see a pair of New Balance sneakers in the crowd. Conversely, if I do not see the New Balance emblem I am elated, temporarily free from the drudgery of my neurosis.

One time a photographer was taking my picture while he

was wearing New Balance sneakers. I told him that I would look much more relaxed and happy if he took off his shoes. Other times I have requested that people change their shoes, and if they do not indulge me I sulk and sit in silent scorn. How mean and spiteful for a company to name a shoe "New Balance." How unfair to the balance impaired! What do they know about balance? Have they ever wiped out into a fruit stand? It is an outrage.

BACK TO WORK: "ARE YOU THE PACEMAKER REPRESENTATIVE?"

By 1989 I had already blasted through several jobs, including my "high-profile" Merrill Lynch job. Little did I know that I had not seen anything yet. In fact, I had about twenty more horrific jobs to go. I felt as though I had exhausted all family and friend connections and was now relegated to my last resort, the biggest crapshoot in town, the impersonal *New York Times* Help Wanted section.

I immediately went to the sales listings. Like most pleasant but highly dysfunctional fuckups with no tangible skills, I was constantly told that I was a "people person" and would make a great salesman or teacher. I can understand salesman, but teacher?

Most of the ads for salespeople in the *NY Times* Help Wanted section claim that they are looking for a bright, articulate "go-getter type" to sell a product that "everyone wants, needs, and can't wait to buy!" This claim is followed by "earn thousands a week" or "earn as much as you want!" Nine times out of ten a person takes this sales job only to discover that no one wants, needs, or will buy the product.

The office of American Universal Press (AUP)—be wary of broad names like this—reeked of scam and high turnover. There were school seats with small folding desktops with standard applications placed on top. This outfit obviously interviewed a lot of people. What stood out was that the place was clouded in smoke; people actually smoked in their offices. Talk about an anachronism.

Ostensibly, AUP was a publishing concern. I did not have a clue about publishing, but I liked the idea of calling my grandfather in Boston to say that I was "in publishing." I would finally be part of the Establishment.

I also observed that I was one of the only white guys in the place. I waited for about an hour (I was obviously being iced) before finally meeting with a slim, well-dressed man who was the president of the company and chain-smoked cigarettes. He had a huge dictionary on his desk and began to tell me how this book sold itself.

At first glance the dictionary was a beautiful, leather-bound reference book. It looked like a book one would see behind a lawyer's desk in a movie. Magnificent in structure and detail (actually made out of cheap nylon), it would look wonderful atop a coffee table.

The president then asked me to talk a little about myself and how I heard about AUP. Enthusiastically—and in hindsight, naïvely—I furnished him with all the information I thought he wanted to know (captain of my cross-country team in high school, et cetera). All the while, the guy was sizing me up to determine if I could drag his huge, cheap Webster's dictionaries to unsuspecting minorities, mostly immigrants, who could be coaxed into believing they would be: a) guaranteeing their child's education by buying one; b) improving their social status. I found AUP marketing tactics to be exploitative and opportunistic, but I reasoned that everyone could use a dictionary. Plus Webster's was a good name.

From Dale Carnegie classes I had taken, I knew that I would have to build up an enthusiasm for a product in order to sell it. The more specific questions I asked about the book, the more the president avoided them and stressed sales tactics instead.

I was "hired" and went through a day of training with a colorful little white Napoleon type named Joey. Joey spent most of the day screaming "This is the book! This is the book!" He completely avoided talking about the qualities of the book. He insisted that we should sell it only in poor neighborhoods or in hospitals to unsuspecting staff members. As an example, he mentioned the owner of a bodega who wanted the book so badly for his family that he paid him in all one-dollar bills. The book went for seventy-nine dollars.

He then explained that if I could make it deep inside a hospital, then the "island nurses" would buy the books like hotcakes because they had credit cards and kids. Apparently, that was my target market—immigrants with credit cards and kids.

Joey also instructed my training group (three young black college kids and me) to stay away from the white supervisors, for they were trouble. He further instructed that if people asked how much it cost, right off the bat we should walk away because they were not serious. (This was actually a good point.)

On my first day Joey brought me to the Hunts Point area of the Bronx, which consisted of only factories and warehouses. Joey told me to try to get into as many buildings as possible and tell employees that they were eligible for a special employee discount.

There I was, a Nichols from a long line of captains of industry and commerce who had actually created some factories, and I was poised to enter into one, unannounced and illegally, to sell a fucking dictionary.

My first few attempts did not go particularly well. Most people were simply apathetic toward my stuttering, sweaty pitch. Other people were not as pleasant. In one factory I managed to elude a security guard and walked into an office where some guys were sitting and talking. I sat down and began my pitch. I told them it was critical that they buy the book for their families. They were respectful until one of the guys asked how I had gotten into the building.

"That's not important. What is important is that you all get this book for your families' future," I replied. At that point he picked up the phone, and a second later an irate security guard viciously threw me out the door.

Now I was getting into it. My adrenaline was stirred up. It became a game. My next stop would be a Coca-Cola plant. At least this was a legitimate outfit. I expected rejection, but lo and behold, I sold a book to the first guy I approached on the loading dock. I then followed sales procedure and used his name to sell more books. Sure enough after an hour, I had sold five goddamn books. It seemed as if everyone wanted one.

I should have stayed on the loading dock. Instead I got cocky and ventured upstairs to the corporate offices. Once there, I noticed a roomful of businessmen waiting for a meeting to begin. My timing was perfect. They all looked like potential customers to me. I was on a roll. Nothing could stop me. Just like the good men downstairs, these would all go down.

I walked confidently to the podium and started my pitch.

"Before your meeting I would like to take the opportunity . . ." I started, slowly beginning to realize the utter absurdity of my position. I began to falter. I began to sweat. I began to stutter. ". . . to offer you a book that as part of your benni-ben- bennnnefit program you are entitled to at half off," I continued.

I was subdued by security. The cops were called. I got off with a warning.

This incident certainly tempered the high I had acquired from my initial sales. When Joey picked me up, I told him that I was not cut out for this stuff, and furthermore it was illegal.

Joey was obviously prepared for this resistance. He had seen it before, and it was a merely a bump in the road for him. Within minutes he had me pumped up to sell again. He was using provocative sales jargon like "Why don't you lose the skirt and quit being a pussy? Do you want to be in sales or not? If you can sell this book, you will be able to sell anything! What, with the first sight of resistance you quit?" It worked.

The next day, Joey brought me to a hospital. In those pre-9/11 days of apathetic security, hospitals were easy to get into. Once inside, Joey told me that the deeper we got into the hospital, the more unsuspecting the staff would be of salesmen; thus they would be more prone to buy the book.

I agreed with Joey, but I balked when he started to push open a door marked for authorized personnel only. Again he started in with the "What are you, a pussy?" stuff. I yielded and followed apprehensively. Once inside the door, Joey went up to a rack of folded clothing and instructed me to put the stuff on. I wore a gown, a hat, and a face mask.

Inside of an hour, we had both sold several books in places like the morgue (I was selling a book while someone was literally working on a body) and the radiology department. I have got to say Joey was good, and it was true that once one nurse showed interest in the book, the rest followed suit. The trick was to jot down or take as many credit card imprints as possible before security was inevitably alerted.

Finally, Joey decided to push the envelope and go into intensive care. Caught in a state of sales euphoria, I was betrayed by my usually ethical instincts. I went in aggressively. Dressed in my gown, I had the nurses interested from the start. They thumbed through the book and looked at the picture section while I pitched them flawlessly, oblivious to the patients behind me who were fighting for dear life.

Next was the operating room. I was doing well there, too. After all, I had been referred by the good nurses and doctors from the intensive care unit.

Unexpectedly, a doctor with blood covering his gown came out from behind a curtain. He pointed to me and asked if I was the pacemaker representative. Now the nurses looked serious. Apparently, in some cases, the pacemaker salesmen had to be present at the time of insertion due to the highly technical nature of the product.

I was on the spot. I looked the doctor right in the eye.

"No," I chirped optimistically, "I am the dictionary salesman."

This time I was arrested and spent one of my many nights in jail.

I should add that the lowest thing I ever did during my limited weeks as a dictionary salesman was unload books on my poor family members, one of whom was my aunt who was recovering from invasive surgery at St. Vincent's Hospital. However, I take some solace in the fact that I gave her a discount.

THE YELLOW SHIRT

I started to go on a lot of interviews after my dictionary career. Unfortunately, I have the tendency to become annoyed by little things that divert my attention away from the task at hand. I am told that many people with LD suffer from a condition known as obsessive-compulsive disorder (OCD). Dreading the worst, those with OCD tend to undermine their own chances for success before the event even takes place. This unfortunate condition tends to rear its ugly head right before an important interview.

Since I drank and drugged my entire way through college, I was unqualified for every possible job out there. I mean, I could break a fax machine just by looking at it.

To disguise my lack of ability, I adopted a superficial power—executive attitude at job interviews. I looked the part because my sister was a vice president of Hugo Boss clothing, and I had expensive suits. To hype myself up I would often go through a ritual in which I would practice pitching a baseball in front of the mirror in a bathroom. (This was awkward in a crowded public restroom.)

I had mastered the perfect smoke-and-mirrors game. I supported the illusion with, quite frankly, a bunch of lies. Most of the time I would get the interviewer talking and then nod intensely at key moments. This formula often worked. I landed jobs for which I was completely unqualified. Around the fifth week, however, the powers that be would realize that they had been had and show me the door.

At any rate, on one particular day, I was pumping myself up for an interview by repeating my "Why not me?" mantra. I was in the midst of putting on my powerhouse clean white starched interview shirt when the top button popped off. Initially, I acted appropriately, simply taking another dress shirt from my closet and putting it on, only slightly aware that the shirt was yellow. As I walked down Second Avenue my mind began, as it always did, to race through huge amounts of negative data, not resting until it found the one hideous morsel of negativity that would bring my house of cards crashing down. That morsel turned out to be the very yellow shirt I had just put on. At first, the voice in my head was very subtle. "Isn't it too bad I simply popped the button off my power broker shirt?" As I walked, I observed other men in suits. Of course, they were wearing nice white shirts. Who would wear a yellow shirt to an interview? How disrespectful of the Establishment. How unprofessional. My anxiety turned into panic. *Now I'll blow the interview*, I thought. *Who would hire someone in a yellow shirt?* I was also becoming aware that the collar on the shirt seemed to be abnormally large. Rather than a short, sharp, clean collar, it was large and cumbersome, suggesting an afternoon of off-track betting.

I bumped into a friend on the street whom I had not seen in years. "What do you think of this shirt I'm wearing?" I asked him. While I tried to come across as confident and calm, I am sure my eyes bespoke my neurosis. In hopes of comforting me, he told me I looked fine.

As I moved on, the issue of the shirt further contaminated my thinking. My world became very narrow. I did not have enough cash on me to buy a new white shirt. On the subway I was surrounded by what seemed to be a sea of white shirts. Even on the elevator, the operator wore a perfectly clean, appropriate white shirt. I am surprised I did not offer to buy the shirt off of him.

Once in the waiting room, I sat down with the other applicants, my competition. We all sat pensively. I imagine the other guys were contemplating their résumés and thinking of ways they could help the company. These were All-American men. They were part of the Establishment.

None of them had a yellow shirt on, or a pink shirt for that matter. Years of guilt and shame poured over me to the point where I became paralyzed. I was a fraud, an impostor. I tried desperately to conceal my negativity, to summon just a little charisma and chutzpah, a little fake bravado.

Somehow it worked. I finally started to relax. *Was I crazy?* I thought. The people at this company were interested in quality of character. Sure, they need presentable, good-looking people who can dress themselves, but they would not care what color shirt a person had on. Just then, a woman came out of the office and said, "Will the man with the yellow shirt please step in?"

TIME FOR SOME RECREATION: THE YACHT

A person who has organizational problems must choose his pas-
times carefully. I am a fishing fanatic, particularly in the fall,
which is the time to catch bluefish and striped bass off Long
Island. Armed with a case of Budweiser, I would go on missions
to catch these extremely easy to catch (when migrating) fish by
paying my way onto a charter fishing boat, surf casting from the
beach, or borrowing/stealing a friend's boat. I would do whatever it took to catch fish.

Let me add parenthetically that, as the captain of a charter
boat myself (and more on this later), I will tell anybody, organi-
zationally fucked up or not, to think twice before buying a boat.
And if staying organized is an issue, I have to warn you: *stay
away!* Boats are all about details. There are a million variables:
radios, wires, fishing equipment, tools, sparkplugs, et cetera. At
the dock if the lines are not tied and coiled a certain way, then
the outgoing tide will come and you will ruin the boat. If the
oil fuel mixture is not vigilantly monitored down to the ounce,
then the engine will fail and you will ruin the boat. If you are
lucky enough to actually get out in the boat, you have to be able
to read the charts because if you cannot, then you might run
aground and you will ruin the boat.

Then there is the intricate buoy system by which you must
abide. Some buoys you have to keep to your right while others
you must keep to your left. This can be difficult for anyone,
but if you are dyslexic it can be so overwhelming that you may
become paralyzed with indecision and end up colliding with the
buoys. Of course, you will *ruin the boat.*

I suppose fishing satisfies some hunter-gatherer instinct in me. Catching fish was a tangible activity that validated me: if I could catch fish, how could I be a loser? Alas, I am afraid that in my drunken years, before I miraculously got good enough at fishing to turn professional, my enthusiasm for it far exceeded my expertise. One time, in fact, my irrational drunken lust for fishing actually had a friend and me swimming for our lives.

At the time, I was house painting for Nichols Enterprises. It was the end of October. A clear blue sky and a temperature of seventy degrees were all it took to spark my fishing interest. I convinced my reluctant friend Steve, who, I might add, is no longer my friend, to pack up his car and head for Westhampton, Long Island, only a two-hour drive away.

It took some work to convince Steve, for he had taken the trip twice before with dismal results each time. (Running out of gas, boat not starting, bad equipment, and worse weather.)

"The blues will be jumping into our hands," I stated emphatically. Like all addicts I could be very persuasive.

Plus, this time I told him that we could use my stepfather's brand-new twenty-eight-foot yacht, complete with radar and outriggers.

The drive down was buoyant (no pun intended) with optimism. It was a beautiful day. When we reached the dock, however, we did notice a very stiff breeze that had not been present when we started out. To anyone even remotely familiar with the sea, wind is a blatant indicator that there are rough conditions ahead. Always—no exceptions: wind = trouble. Nevertheless, we had traveled two hours, bought bait, and picked up a case of beer. A little bit of wind was not going to foil our fishing extravaganza.

We piled our stuff into my stepfather's boat, and though the choppy waters in the harbor tempered our enthusiasm a little, a couple of beers turned us, or at least me, into a fearless old salt and wiped away most of my apprehension.

As we approached the inlet, which led to the Atlantic, we made a few observations: one, there were no other boats out, which seemed odd for such a beautiful day; and two, a number of red flags hung from flag poles. (Now I know they were small-craft warnings.) The choppy water in the harbor was only a prelude to what was to come.

Moreover, it is an understatement to say that the inlet looked rough. Sheltered from the wind, the harbor was placid compared to the inlet, which led out to the ocean. Immense swells lurked beyond the waves crashing in front of us.

A quick glance at Steve was all it took to recognize his concern. But I was not going to turn back. I also remembered hearing that once a boat enters a rough inlet, it should not be turned around because it could be broadsided by an incoming wave, take on water, and sink. Many a boat has met this fate. This gave me an excuse to press on into the open ocean where, a mile or so out, I knew the swells, though large, would be less threatening, and, more important, hold fish.

By now, my obviously frightened companion was protesting my decision to press on.

"We have to turn around!" Steve demanded.

"At this point, we're pretty much fucked anyway! There's no turning back," I told him, summoning as much confidence as possible. I concentrated on the elusive undulating horizon.

The waves were immense and punishing. Some must have been close to ten feet. Each one was fraught with peril. We rode a wave up, waited for what seemed an eternity at the crest, and then fell freely into the valley of another. This happened over and over again while I was doing everything I could to keep the boat straight. With every wave, gallons and gallons of water crashed over the boat and into the cockpit.

When riding up the waves the boat was at an almost ninety-degree angle. The only thing holding me to the boat was the steering wheel. My desperate friend clung to a handle for his life. Food, equipment, beer, and anything else not tied down all disappeared into the sea. Each swell dramatically shook the structure of the boat, testing its integrity with every thrashing. When a break in the waves gave me opportunity, I picked up a long piece of rope and tied it around my waist. I instructed my friend to tie it around his belt so that, in case we got swept overboard we could find each other. When I suggested this, he shouted back angrily, "I would rather tie myself to the anchor than your drunk ass!"

Finally, we made it out to calmer waters where the swells were still massive but less threatening than the thunderous crashing waves in the inlet. As they were not breaking anymore, they were gentle giants. Even as we sat there soaking wet and rolling about in the high seas, I entertained the thought of dropping a line overboard to try to land a bluefish. When I suggested this to my delirious and disenchanted friend, he commanded me to radio for help. I told him that you were only supposed to radio for help if you were in distress and we were not in distress. "We are in fucking distress, there is no way we will make it through that inlet, radio for help!" he shrieked.

Not having lost all reason completely, I tried to use the elaborate high-tech radio. It was dead. At this point, I thought I could safely turn the boat around and, keeping the boat true, ride the waves back through the inlet to the safety of the harbor.

I was about to try this maneuver, which, judging by my inexperience at handling a boat, would have been catastrophic for sure, when the engine conked out. Like the radio, it was dead.

I considered going through the academic motions of removing the engine cover and looking at the engine, but, paralyzed by technology, I knew there was no point. I knew nothing. I spent too much time at tennis camp and no time with a wrench in my hand like a real man. We were sitting ducks, dead in the water.

The tide pulled us slowly toward our inevitable doom among the crashing waves and jagged rocks of the inlet. Steve, I remember, was drenched in his red Patagonia all-weather gear, camouflage pants, and Timberland boots, and he clutched his grandfather's fishing rod, which obviously had sentimental value, for some morsel of comfort.

In preparation for the worst, I told Steve to take off his clothes, and he did so mechanically. We had no life preservers.

The sun was shining, but it was cold. Luckily, it was an incoming tide and we were pushed down past the inlet to a beach area and escaped being crushed on the rocks of the jetties, but the waves were still huge, unyielding, and breaking about ten seconds apart. For about an hour we drifted closer to the beach. A quarter mile away from shore the swells turned into pounding waves.

If the tide and luck cooperated, we might be able to swim to shore after hitting the water.

"What do we do now?" Steve asked. He stood there shivering and almost naked in his Fruit of the Looms.

We were at least two hundred yards from the shore. An enormous wave was bearing down on us. At this point, I gave the command every sea captain prays he will never have to give.

"Jump!" I yelled. He did. I followed. And the wave crashed over the impotent vessel.

We were now completely at the mercy of the sea. There was no use fighting, except for the occasional gasp for air between waves. I surrendered.

As if this were not bad enough, I do remember that I jumped from the wrong side of the boat—in front of it rather than behind it. I felt the entire boat go over me and smash into the sand bar, the boat just missing me. I have never been so in touch with my mortality.

Somehow, I ended up on the beach (Dune Road), out of breath and a little cut up. I had been spared! To add to my gratitude, I looked up to see my abused friend Steve, whom I had completely forgotten about, walking toward me in his underwear about fifty yards down the beach.

The cost of getting the ruined boat off the sea floor was over ten grand; luckily, insurance paid for it all.

A TRIP TO THE DOCTOR

After the boat incident my family insisted that I go to a therapist immediately. I went to a place called Family Counseling Services in Manhattan. A doctor or counselor or shrink (whatever the hell he was) told me that my behavior was "impulsive" and "reckless" and suggested that amphetamines (Ritalin, Delirium, Cylert) could make me more focused and therefore more civilized. He told me that if I had been more focused, I would have been engaged in my work and would not have had the impulse to drop everything and drive two hours to go fishing.

I understood what he told me, but I had read that the drug ecstasy was amphetamine based, and the thought of taking a drug in the same family as ecstasy terrified me. (In a sick way it intrigued me, too.) My intuition told me that my nervous system could not handle the punishment of any more stimulants.

Plus, I knew I was an addict. I am sure the drugs could have made me more focused and civilized, but at that time I thought that I might be able to get the same thing by going the holistic route via diet, exercise, and meditation.

A friend suggested that I see a hypnotist. For seventy-five bucks the hypnotist told me that I was traveling down a babbling brook. As I traveled down the babbling brook in an inner tube (I had a choice of canoe, raft, or inner tube), all I could think about was the seventy-five bucks I had to hand over after my excursion. Don't you think for seventy-five dollars he could have broken out some monkey juice?

Yoga was also supposed to help improve clarity. I went to one session at a gym in Greenwich Village that consisted of mostly good-looking women. Though I did appreciate the breathing techniques, I was alarmingly inflexible. I eventually just sat there and tried to conceal my hard-on.

BACK TO WORK:
ON WITH THE SHOW

With my nerves shot by my brief time in dictionary sales, I looked around for something more benign. A job with less stress, a steady paycheck, and more consistent with my (dopamine-deficient) abilities. My stepfather knew an older lady named Ray who was the head usher at the Walter Kerr Theater on Broadway. While being an usher was certainly not a "glamour job," I have always embraced the theory that all jobs have dignity. I figured if I could get the job, I would try it for a while. It was also appealing because there might be some health benefits attached.

My first day at the theater, I was approached by what appeared to be a nice, charming old Irishwoman in her seventies. When I told her I was there to see Ray about work, she abruptly told me, "The asshole is upstairs in the dressing room."

I went up to the dressing room and cautiously peeped my head in the door. At first, all I saw was dense smoke and a bunch of older ladies sitting around a table.

"What do you want!" one of the ladies belched.

I quickly found out that most of the Broadway theaters were run by older Irishwomen who were a blast to be with but had gutter mouths. Ray was no exception.

"Oh yeah, you're Mike Gibbons's stepson," she said. Then, very secretively, she whispered to me in a raspy whisky Pall Malls smoker's voice, as if she were giving me a hot stock tip. "You can start tonight. Be here at seven p.m. sharp and look good. Black shoes and pants. White button-down. Black tie. Flashlight if you got it, and if you don't we will give you one."

Of course, I showed up late and disheveled. My cotton shirt and pants were wrinkled. I was wearing sneakers and had no tie.

As instructed, I went straight up to the locker room to find Ray, who then told me for the first of many times to get my "union dues" in as soon as possible and then introduced me to the floor manager, Betty Ann.

Incidentally, all women in the Broadway playhouses seem to have two first names, one of which is always Ann: Betty Ann, Mary Ann, Judith Marie Ann, et cetera. There were also some other classic older names in there, real anachronisms like Gertrude, Ingrid, and Agnes. Let me just say that I loved these women. They were hardworking decent folk from whom I derived strength, and, hopefully, character. I ended up becoming great friends with many of them. Betty Ann was supposed to show me the layout of the theater.

"In about an hour, the entire place will be crammed with

bitchy homos," she told me. The show that was presently playing at the Walter Kerr Theater was *Love! Valour! Compassion!*,
and it was one of only a few plays then that involved homosexuality.

She then went on to furnish me with the fundamentals: how
to seat people, the order of rows, the location of the bathrooms,
and so forth. Unfortunately, I was almost completely tuned out.
I just sat there kind of nodding. On my first night, a Tuesday, I
believe I caught a nap. I was put up in the balcony and there was
not much to do. The next day, I had to report in at the theater
at one p.m. for the Wednesday matinee. Again, I was briefed by
Betty Ann. Again, I retained nothing. All I knew was that the
odd numbers were on one end of the row while the evens were
on the other. Seats in the one hundreds were in the middle. The
rows on the balcony began at A and ended at H.

The Walter Kerr Theater is one of the oldest theaters in
Manhattan. It is a beautiful and elegantly appointed space, but
the architects did not have the elderly in mind when they designed it. A billy goat would have trouble scaling the balcony.
Pitched at nearly a ninety-degree angle, I was instructed to
escort anyone who needed help to a seat. At a matinee, this
meant senior citizens, who comprised just about all of the customers. I loved doing it at first. I love all old people, and I really
felt as though I was being of service.

That particular day, it was not only just old people but also
a lot of school groups. Realizing that I did not have time to seat
all these people, I decided to expedite matters by continuing to
help the elders while simply pointing the students to the general
direction of their seats. Of course, not one of the brats listened
to me, and they sat wherever they damn well pleased.

There were a couple of rows of conspicuously unfilled seats, but I felt certain that everyone would be more or less seated and happy by the time the curtain finally went up. I quickly found out that "more or less" did not cut it. Two minutes into the show Betty Ann informed me that a busload of people had just arrived. I was shocked that they would let them in so late. Where was I going to seat these people? What was to follow can only be described as unmitigated pandemonium. I began to panic, and my dyslexia went off the charts.

People yelled and fought. Other ushers came to my assistance, but it was too late. The performance had been so severely interrupted by the ruckus in the balcony that five minutes into the play I am surprised the curtain was not lowered. I had made my mark on Broadway.

Though I was accosted with unspeakable vulgarities by the staff, somehow I was not fired. I remained an usher for three more years.

I loved all of the plays and enjoyed my naps in the balcony. I also relished my breaks during which I would walk to Times Square, where a black evangelist perched on a metal box would preach while dressed as a superhero and insult unsuspecting white tourists from the Midwest who had gathered around expecting some sort of freak show, perhaps, or a dance or a song of some sort, only to be called "white Sodomites" by an angry black man and then flee.

The only embarrassing moment in my ushering career occurred when I was forced to seat my old girlfriend from high school and her boyfriend. Keep in mind, I wore a bow tie and a cheap polyester double knit shirt and carried a flashlight.

"Hi! Glad see to you. You're in the fifth row center. Enjoy the show!" I then peered down from my station to see her gesturing with her hands, obviously trying to explain to her boyfriend how in the world she ever went out with the likes of me.

I was assigned to the musical *Cats* for five weeks straight. Did I want to take a gun to my head, hearing "Memories" over and over? Absolutely. Plus, after ten years on Broadway, the cats were probably the most apathetic lot of cats you could find. The show was on life support. All the tickets were half price—no original actors were left. They were clearly phoning in their performances. The costumes were as weathered as the actors' faces.

Cats was to close the next month. However, one time right after intermission something happened to make that night particularly interesting. What appeared to be a homeless woman merged with the audience members. She entered the theater and, carrying two brown shopping bags, walked onstage with the cats, who were just assuming their places. The lady walked all around the set. The audience thought that it was part of the play, that this apparently was how act two really began. To be honest, it did look natural. She really complemented the set. (In case you are one of the six people who missed seeing *Cats*, the set is a dreary junkyard.) The cats began to improvise off her; walking up to her, and smelling her and brushing by her. It was a wonderful moment of improvisation. Finally, one of the cats coaxed the woman off the stage.

I did finally pay my union dues. The union office was located in a five-story walk-up in Hell's Kitchen. I think I owed three hundred bucks. I knocked on the door and sure enough I heard the familiar "Who the hell is it?" I walked in to see some old Irish broads playing cards. I threw the money into the middle of the table, where I figured it would end up as the day's "kitty" and walked right back out. As I left, I heard one old Irish broad. "It's about fucking time!"

UNEMPLOYMENT

If you have a learning disability get ready for long droughts of joblessness. These spells are brutal on one's self-esteem. Unemployed people have to carry around the stigma that comes from being unemployed, but what is interesting is that unemployed people are often busier than employed people.

Also, if I may say a word about something I call "the hundred-dollar gig." The hundred-dollar gig has been the same price for years. It is the standard amount that day losers get for doing shitty jobs (house painting, moving, digging ditches, what have you). My beef with "the hundred-dollar gig" is that the amount never budges. I never have someone call me up to say, "Hey Jeff, can you help me lay some cement today? It will only take eight hours or so and I will pay you $125.00!" *No*, it's always $100.00. Decades go by, wars are fought, new technology is invented, but the hundred-dollar gig stays the same. In 1990, a gallon of milk and a gallon of gas were 99 cents. The hundred-dollar gig was a hundred-dollar gig. Today, a gallon of gas and a gallon of milk are close to $3.50, but the hundred-dollar gig is still . . .

Unemployed people are constantly sitting in other people's apartments waiting for the cable guy, the plumber, and the rug delivery. Show me a guy driving down a street desperately holding on to a mattress that has come undone on the roof of his old car, and I will show you an unemployed guy. Chances are, the owner of that mattress is downloading porn at his office. When performing other people's chores, I recommend a strict "no moving" policy.

During one spell, I had at least a full year of total unemployment. Not only did I not have a job, but I also did not want one. I went on the occasional obligatory interview to placate my parents, but most days were spent as follows: wake up around ten; make a huge pot of coffee so dense and potent that my hair sticks up; stare at a tremendous heap of unopened mail until panic-stricken (my typical mail consists of bills, subpoenas, warrants, and summonses). Once sufficiently wired on caffeine, head to the gym and lift weights for three straight hours.

Lifting weights was a great activity for me because it provided a routine. What I found interesting was that while my apartment resembled ground zero, at the gym I would always neatly stack the weights in their appropriate places after using them. Pretty good for a guy who never washed a dish.

Anyone who lifts weights knows that to get results it is vital to vary the workout: upper body one day, lower body the next, and cardio the day after that. This way the muscles have time to heal. I, of course, repeated the same workout. I worked out the same body parts day after day (I always wondered why I never got any bigger), swinging around the weights incorrectly like a mental patient, almost exclusively using my lower lumbar as an axis.

Instructors and concerned fellow gym members would often approach and tell me that I was lifting improperly and that I could seriously hurt myself. To their well-intentioned but unsolicited advice, I would take offense. I would indignantly thank them and continue on with my unconventional workout.

After three hours or so, I would come home with the false feeling that I had accomplished something. Physically, I felt like a construction worker after a long day, exhausted yet content and relaxed. Piles of bills still littered the floor of my apartment, but now the sight of them was not as disturbing. Lifting weights had given me a false sense of accomplishment and stability. I would then gorge myself on junk food, watch TV all night, and repeat the same thing the next day.

(I just had the realization that life is all about paperwork. Details and tasks are endless, from the motor vehicle department to taxes to paying bills. Everyone is constantly doing domestic chores just to avoid being buried by paperwork. This is fine if you are getting laid. If you are getting laid, you will take on any task with a spring in your step. Even a trip to the dentist, suddenly, is not such a drag. However, if you are not getting laid, life is just exhausting.)

THE ART OF DECEPTION

People with learning disabilities often compensate for them by becoming deceptive and evasive. For two years I snuck into gyms in Manhattan. I did it with such precision that it was almost an art form.

I started out sneaking into the YMCA. Ys are easy places to sneak into because the building is usually turn-of-the-century, and they have an abundance of entrances and staircases. Some doors have emergency signs on them signifying that an alarm will go off if opened, but trust me, most of the time the alarm is disconnected. So live a little and push that door open. If nothing else, it will give you a good adrenaline rush.

After a couple of years of sneaking into the Y, however, my conscience, which had been happily dormant for many years, started to rear its ugly head. (I wonder how many men have been ruined by their consciences.) The fact that a good portion of the membership money went to programs for inner-city children began to wear me down. Eventually, I gave the YMCA a couple of hundred dollars and moved on.

The next gym I targeted was the Reebok Sports Club. At the time, it was the most exclusive and high-priced club in the city, complete with palm trees and celebrity members. So of course I felt entitled to sneak in. Usually I would just kind of slide in behind other members. (Again, it is harder than it looks; deception is a cultivated art.) When this tactic was not possible, I would give the person at the desk, usually an aspiring actor from Indiana who had been in NYC for about a week, a made-up number as I passed by. By the time the person had entered the number and a picture of a sixty-year-old grandmother appeared on the screen, I was already working out.

Another tactic I used was the cruder "blast-by approach." I would tell the person at the desk that I had left something in the locker room, or I needed to buy something at the boutique. This tactic ultimately betrayed me when I told a young woman at the desk that I was on my way to the lost and found. I suppose she had seen me before and was onto me. I heard her yelling after me, "Sir, excuse me! Excuse me!"

My ignoring her must have put her in a real rage because she sent a search party after me. At first, security went right by me in the locker room, assuming that because they had seen me before I must be a member. I took my clothes off and brought my stuff with me to the shower. Who is going to bother a naked man in the shower?

I was wrong. Since I was the only guy in the locker room at the time, security deduced that I was "the one." They approached me in the shower and told me to get dressed and come with them. It was embarrassing for everyone involved. Escorted past the upscale cafeteria on the way out, I restrained myself from shrieking "Is it because I am a Jew and gay that you are throwing me out?"

"HAVE YOU BEEN CLAPPING?"

Around this time my alleged Tourette's syndrome became more pronounced. I was living in an apartment in Greenpoint, Brooklyn, when I got an awkward call from a guy named Mark, from whom I was subletting the apartment. Mark was a nice guy, which made the call profoundly worse. Mark had already made me privy to the fact that the landlord did not like me much. Apparently, the landlord had seen the abominable way I lived. He had also complained that I walked down the stairway too fast, that I never recycled, and that once I had shorted out the entire building when I tried to plug in a powerful air conditioner that the building's electrical system could not accommodate.

All these problems Mark was able to handle. But this particular call was of a more disturbing nature. It was such an uncomfortable issue that Mark had a tough time getting to it. He kind of babbled on a bit about how he had heard that I slept on the fire escape once. (I did, but it was around 110 degrees in the apartment at the time, and I had no AC.) Then he mentioned that he had once again received complaints about my going down the stairs too fast.

But I could tell by the inflection in his voice that there was something else that he had to address but was reluctant to do so. Some other huge domestic faux pas I had made. I began to explain that I would try to go a little slower on the stairs when Mark interrupted.

"Have you been clapping?" he blurted.

"What?" I responded.

"I have received complaints that you have been clapping in the apartment," Mark went on. I was about to deny it and protest the inquiry when I realized that I had, indeed, been clapping.

Sure enough, when I get really excited or I am engaged in some sort of fantasy usually involving sports, I start to either leap around the apartment or sit in a chair rocking back and forth and impulsively clapping. My clapping was not the familiar applause type of clapping people are accustomed to after a speech or a recital. My clapping was shorter, more abrupt, and very intense. Just a couple of real quick up-tempo claps, maybe three in a row. (CLAPCLAPCLAP.)

I now see how this activity concerned my neighbors, who already found me bizarre. One doctor suggested that the clapping is part of my "impulsive" outbursts and is consistent with Tourette's. But, at least, I think going CLAPCLAPCLAP is better than bellowing "CUNTMOTHERFUCKER" like the afflicted frequently do.

I was eventually thrown out of the apartment, not because of the clapping, although I am sure that helped, but because I had too many people staying with me. I had allowed an unemployed friend to live there, and she, a charismatic person, somehow managed to get me to agree to let her friend move in as well.

While at the time I was outraged, I now consider what followed a strategic move worthy of a chess grand master: the girl contacted Mark behind my back and convinced him to let her take over the apartment. When I told the girls that it was time to pack up, they essentially told me to speak for myself.

SUBHUMAN

Of all the jobs out there, I believe there are few other job that requires/demands organizational skills like that of a public school teacher. From a teacher's first day to the last, he or she is buried in paperwork. If you were dyslexic and a new teacher in NYC then you may as well get an apartment close to the Board of Education in Brooklyn, because you were going to be there *all the time.* Not a day goes by when a teacher does not have to fill out some kind of form.

God forbid you have a learning disability because you must write legibly: on the board, notes to parents, notes to principals, and notes to students. In short, you spend your entire first year writing notes and yelling "Who threw that?!"

Having been unemployed for some time, I finally yielded to the chorus of people who told me that since "kids like you and all" I should be a schoolteacher. It is funny how "burnouts" always seem to have their career opportunities ultimately dwindled down to becoming teachers, or artists, or Zamboni operators.

The year was 1990. Mayor David Dinkins was in office; the country was in a full recession, and the crack epidemic was at its peak. Out of thirty kids in a third-grade classroom at least half were in foster care. Many children were being raised by their grandparents, who, God bless them, rose to the occasion. I was told that many New York City public schools, in a perpetual state of desperation for teachers with a pulse, would be willing to hire a person full time who was not state certified. All the perks like health benefits and summers off would be included if you were willing to substitute teach.

I went down to the Board of Education's office in Brooklyn. I am not going to sugarcoat it: while there are some exceptions, most of the people who showed up at that office, myself included, had already rifled through a shitload of jobs. Not many people wake up after graduating from Harvard and say to themselves "Maybe I would make a good substitute teacher."

If you are signing up to be a NYC sub, you are one bad career decision away from a trailer home. When you sign up to be a sub, you are surrendering. You are raising the white flag and walking over to the "war is over and I lost" camp.

Subs have no representation, no union. Consequently, the only support they have is the encouragement they get from each other in the hallways.

"Who do you have today?"

"Ow, they're horrible!"

"Who do you have?"

"Ow, they are even worse!"

"Can you believe that seventh-grade science class!"

There is no real solidarity among substitute teachers and no real control over students. You do not know the little monsters' names, and you cannot give grades, so you are powerless. Eventually, you do not care. All you want to do is keep them in the room so you can get your hundred bucks.

Not only do the kids disrespect you, but the full-time teachers also love watching you go down in flames. If you fail, and you will, it enables them to say things to their principal like, "You think I'm doing a bad job, look at that sub across the hall from me. He can't even keep the students in the room and they call him Rain Man."

Unless you are an "A list" sub, one who is given advance notice of work, you spend a restless night in terror, wondering if a principal will call in the morning. If a principal does call, you debate whether you should go in because, of course, on the day you really do not want to get up, the principal does, in fact, call. It is truly a miserable existence.

It is even more tormenting if you get not one, but two phone calls. If you decide not to go in at all, going back to bed feels great. When you wake up, however, your self-esteem takes a vicious beating. Problems begin when you live in Queens and a school from the Bronx calls first. Not knowing if another school will call, you say you can make it. Grudgingly, you dress yourself and start out the door for the long pilgrimage to the Bronx when the school across the street from you calls to see if you are available. If you are saddled with a conscience, as I am unfortunately (sometimes), you will go to the first school that calls.

Though the kids can be little shits, more often they are the upside to substitute teaching. Once I asked a student if he knew the word *climate*. He told me it was "what you did to a fence."

While there are charming things said by kids that are truly

funny, there are plenty of other less charming and less funny things said by kids.

"Mr. Nichols, you're a nigger!" a kid said to me once. I was not sure how to answer him, so I smiled blankly.

Any substitute teacher in New York City should be ready to hear the n-word often. One of my favorite NYC comedians, who also was a NYC teacher, Gerry Red Wilson, used to say in his act that he once asked one of his kids who Ben Franklin was, to which the student replied that he was the "nigger who discovered electricity!" I suppose he got partial credit.

The day my teaching license came in the mail I called all the good public schools in Manhattan. They instructed me to send in my résumé and they would schedule me for an interview. That was far too much work for me, so I randomly called a school in the South Bronx. I was told to come in immediately.

I was full of optimism when I got to the large elementary school. I had found my calling: to be of service to kids. I would help kids. I would be a beacon of light for these kids. I would be a white knight in the South Bronx.

The assistant principal, in fact everyone who worked in the hectic office, seemed to be glad to see me. I suppose it was because I was male and I had a pulse. After all, kids always need a good male role model and, more important, a disciplinarian. Boy, were these people going to be disappointed.

I was told that the principal would meet with me soon and was ushered into a waiting room, which was tiny and barren but for a single antidrug poster on the wall. You know the one: the egg sizzling in a frying pan with the inscription below that reads, "This Is Your Brain on Drugs." At first, it did not bother me, but as time passed, I became fixated on the poster. It began to consume me. Like cancer, the poster began to gnaw away at my positive "can do" attitude. My mood plummeted. Twenty minutes later, I was rocking in my seat like a true psycho, wondering, *What the fuck am I doing here! I am a complete burnout dyslexic who is a little light on bone marrow. What can I teach these kids? What wisdom can I give? How to make a bong out of an apple? Or possibly, how to stare at a woman until she is uncomfortable?*

I was drowning in a sea of self-manufactured negativity. I was sweating profusely, shaking, and about to assume the fetal position when the principal finally arrived. He was a pleasant man, albeit tired and frazzled looking. He had the kind of "I'm retiring next year" look to him. Apparently, he did not notice—or more probably chose to ignore—my obviously troubled state.

"Hi. I'm glad you are here," he said, shaking my clammy hand. He asked no questions. I followed him down a hallway dense with rowdy screaming kids who were oblivious to the principal's presence. Not a good sign.

"Unfortunately, the fifth-grade class I am going to give you is a little difficult to control. They have been through three certified teachers already." It was only October. As he brought me to the door of the classroom, I tried in vain to summon some positive slogans that I had learned in AA. The principal opened the door to reveal forty kids. Many were wrestling, many drawing on the blackboard. some were crying, others were laughing. The principal asked me my name again.

"This is Mr. Nichols. He is your teacher today. Please respect him." He then wished me luck and whispered, "Don't smile, no matter what. And keep them in the room. That's all you have to do—just keep them in the room."

As if to see what I was made of, the class got quiet for a moment after the principal left. The calm before the storm. Again, I had no official training at that time, but I have learned that teaching in NYC comes down to a case of whether you "got it" or you "don't got it." I am not even sure what "it" is or even how one "got" it. I would guess it is some magical cocktail of compassion, organizational skills, patience, and certainly discipline. All I know is I "don't got it." My problem was that I got really excited as I looked at the kids. I saw them all as potential friends. I wanted them to like me. I really thought that we were going to get a lot accomplished.

"So," I began, "my name is Mr. Nichols—"

"Pickles!" one kid instantly screeched. There it was, my first challenge. In hindsight I should have driven a stake through that kid's heart, thereby establishing respect, but of course I did nothing. Seeing that I did not care, the class laughed. I remember what the principal had told me about the importance of not smiling, so I continued.

"Who can tell me, by raising your hand, what you all have been studying?" One very heavyset girl raised her hand. When I called on her she pointed to the girl next to her and said "All I know is that bitch needs a Tic Tac!" Again the class cracked up. And so did I. I could not help it. Her delivery was perfect. We all laughed. But I had broken the code of not smiling and now I had to pay a severe price. I had now become the biggest kid in the class.

"Sit down! Shut up! Put that down! No, you can't all go to

the bathroom at once! Who threw that? What's your name? Will someone please untie me?" I screamed all morning.

During my lunch break, I went out to a bodega. I knew that I was going into battle in the afternoon, and I needed ammo: M&Ms. The only way I was going to be able to keep these kids in the room for the rest of the day was via bribery. I bought about a dozen bags of candy.

The rest of the day was spent playing endless rounds of Simon Says. (Winner gets candy!) When that grew unbearable (kids began to collapse), I put a bunch of numbers on the board and said whoever guesses the number gets a bag. This seemed to keep the wolf pack at bay for a while. During the last half hour things degenerated into my simply handing out bags of M&Ms to the quietest kid. (Pedagogical experts were turning in their graves.)

At ten of three I knew I was in trouble. These kids were about to make a premature run for the door. And I was down to one bag of M&Ms. I knew I had to hold onto that bag, because it was my last resource. For five minutes I sat in front of the door literally pushing the little monsters back. They pushed me and kicked my shins. One little brat shot Elmer's glue all over me. Finally, sensing certain mutiny at five minutes to three, I launched the last bag over the hostile mass into the back of the room. A massive pileup ensued. As in any battle, there were a few casualties: a chipped tooth, a bloody nose, and some hurt feelings, but I had done my job. I had kept them in the room.

Somehow, I was invited back the next day. This time I was given a different class. They were another tough bunch, but this time I was prepared.

I walked in with a stern expression, put my name on the

blackboard, ignoring kids calling out "Pickles" followed by the obligatory laughter. (My plan was to up the bribery stakes.) I then told them that I was primarily an art teacher (lie) and that I had also just spoken to the gym teacher (lie) and he said if they were all good, I could take them to the gym during last period (lie). I also said that I had a lot of fun games for the class to play (lie) and a "shark video" to watch (lie) if the class was good and finished its math that morning. I proceeded to write all the stuff that I claimed to have on the board. When it got too noisy, I would put a check by one of the activities. Three checks and the class could not do that particular activity (like watching the fictitious shark video).

At the end of the day, I was at the board. Most of the activities had three checks and a line through them signifying that the kids had blown it. The only one left on the board without three checks was the gym option. It had two checks.

"The next time one of you little rats throws something, there will be no gym!" I screamed, "That's it! *No gym!*" At this point I did not care that I was losing what was left of my mental faculties.

What pissed me off about that particular school is that I got no backup. (Like the soldier trapped in a hole under heavy fire in war, I was constantly on the phone requesting assistance.) Every once in a while I thought that I was getting some help. One time two women came into the classroom. They were well-dressed professional types. I naively thought that backup had finally arrived. The women ignored me as well as all the screaming kids and just took the two kids who were in wheelchairs out for physical therapy. I was outraged. Those kids were fine sitting in those wheelchairs; they were not the ones causing problems.

Why couldn't they have taken Jean, who had just stabbed Janelle in the head with a pencil?

Eventually, I got blown out of that school. The kids caught on to my apathy and incompetence.

Even if I had never touched a drug in my life, I could never have handled being a full-time teacher. My lack of organizational skills in conjunction with my reading and spelling problems and abominable handwriting made it too difficult. I had problems simply managing my own paperwork, let alone the records of forty kids. Again, teaching in the inner city, from what I can tell, is about whether you "got it." I now suspect that "it" is really classroom control.

Not knowing what else to do, I pressed on in the field. Sure, one school had fired me, but there were plenty of other schools I could try. And, even if I exhausted all of the schools in the Bronx, I could always try Brooklyn or Staten Island. I found one school in the South Bronx where the principal, once again, made the erroneous assumption that I could control the class because I was a man. Obviously, the principal miscalculated my abilities. She offered me a job instantly.

Though I was hired as a full-time teacher, I was not given my own classroom. Rather, I was given a "cluster" program. A cluster teacher, like a sub, goes from room to room, relieving other teachers for forty-five-minute spells at a time. The difference between a cluster teacher (I know, you would think that there would be a better name for it, but I thought about it and concluded that there really isn't) and a sub is that a cluster teacher is given some sort of curriculum like a math or health program. These programs are not in lieu of normal class work, but are a supplement to it.

My program was the multicultural reading program, which was designed to expose kids to other worlds through literature. I was supposed to assemble the kids in an orderly fashion and then read to them various folklore and literature from different lands.

The problem was that I have something like a fifth-grade reading level, and when I have to read aloud, that fifth-grade reading level plummets three grades. I sat there on a stool, stuttering and sweating, while the kids waited and wondered if I was about to throw up. The good part is that the cluster teacher had very little accountability, no grades, no homework. The bad part is that the kids saw the period as a chance to wreak absolute havoc.

From day one I had no control over my classes. I walked into the classroom hoping that the teacher would stay awhile. They tried to help sometimes, making threats and telling me if kids misbehaved I should write their name on the board. Within minutes of the teacher's departure, there was mayhem. The first thing that always happened when the teacher left and I entered is everyone decided they needed to feed the fish, gerbil, or hamster and/or water the plant. If I said no, the class looked at me as if I were a vicious killer.

Then everyone would want to go to the bathroom. I told them they could go but only one at a time. No one followed this rule.

"I am warning you two—don't go out that door or I will call the office," I warned in vain. "I will call your parents! Don't go out that door!" Always, the students paused, looked at me, judged my resolve, and then called my bluff. They always left. They knew that I would not call the office because that would make me look bad.

Toward the middle of the semester, I started to enjoy the

chaos, particularly during lunch duty. Three other apathetic and broken teachers and I were in charge of some three hundred children eating lunch. One guy screamed into an electric bullhorn (he was actually good) while I walked around in a daze, occasionally tripping a kid or giving him a horsey bite for good sport. Needless to say, the possibly biggest food fight in Bronx public school history broke out under my watch. The shepherd's pie was so thick that one could not see across the room.

One time the principal was supposed to observe me teaching my program. In shell shock, I had forgotten about the appointment and tried to pull something together at the last minute. I remembered that a new teacher, also nuts and struggling, had just been given a globe by her parents for her birthday.

Now, since I was supposed to be teaching "multicultural studies," I figured I could wing the class by playing some foreign music. (I had a cassette player and a lot of tapes.) My intentions were to play the music and then point to its country of origin on my friend's globe.

In the end, the principal never showed up, and the globe was turned into an international soccer ball. I shamefully instructed a kid to simply drop off the bent and mangled globe in front of the teacher's door with an apology note, knock hard, and then take off.

I made it to May, but I was eventually fired from that job as a multicultural cluster teacher after yet another class had trampled over me, getting out early. (I had failed to keep them in the room.) My name was called over the PA. I was being requested to report to the principal's office. The gig was up.

Still, when the principal told me she was giving me two week's notice, I went through the exercise of asking why. She was prepared for that question. She pulled out a rap sheet a mile long.

"Gambling with students. Bribing students. Mentioning your 'balls' in class—"

"That is totally out of context," I interrupted.

But she continued, ignoring me.

"—Saying 'fuck' and 'shit' and 'shut the fuck up.' Referring to students as 'little bastards.' Playing Simon Says for two straight hours. Asking students 'Why do you have to be such assholes?' Using the word 'nigger.' Hanging kids by their underwear. Playing with dice. Wrestling with students and giving them 'horsey bites.'" (She looked up at me on that one, obviously not knowing what a "horsey bite" was.) "Encouraging and arranging food fights in the lunch room." She paused and adjusted her glasses. "Need I go on?"

I got an official "U" for Unsatisfactory; no one gets a "U" from the Board of Education. "U" or no, I still occasionally substitute teach today.

Ten of my fifteen years substitute teaching were spent in New York City elementary and middle schools. Everywhere I went, my only job, the only job of any substitute teacher, was to keep the children in the room. I had always feared teaching in high schools because of the possible violence, until a friend of mine alerted me to the fact that subbing is much easier in high school for the simple reason that the bad kids don't show up. I took this friend's word as true and signed up for a high school assignment in the Bronx. In fact, there were no behavior problems. The bad kids did not show up. Actually, no one showed up. Well, maybe three or four kids who ended up leaving after a while anyway. It is a very sad, seemingly hopeless predicament.

Truancy is not the real problem with high schools, though. The real problem, not just in the inner city but everywhere, is that sex oozes out of every nook and cranny in the high schools. Places of secondary education reek of sex. I switched to high schools in 2002, also known as The Year of the Thong and Low-Low-Rise Jeans. A deadly combo indeed—the kind of combination that could drive a man to tears.

Every girl had them. The jeans were so low that they barely covered the pubic line. Living on Long Island for a spell, I took a job out at East Hampton High School. I would walk down the hallway, trying not to notice the colorful strings that were obviously crammed up these underage girls' asses. Getting caught staring would have been humiliating (and possibly felonious), but at the same time, I defend myself: maybe I would not have been staring at someone's daughter's ass if she had pulled her pants up a bit. Biology is biology. Case closed.

To effectively deal with the responsibilities of parent-teacher conferences, papers to grade, and accountability in general, full-time teachers have built-in defense mechanisms to keep from falling into the throes of lust. A sub, on the other hand, is almost always expected to be a loser, so gawking a bit goes with the territory. Right?

I was very careful not to stare. I cannot think of anything more embarrassing than a teenage girl shrieking out in class, "Mr. Nichols was staring at my tits!" This, of course, never really happened. I am not a pervert (as far as you know). Truth be told, I was never all that lustful; I like kids and I want to see them do well. Really. The ones society must watch out for are the quiet male teachers, the ones who would quickly point out what a loser I am, especially the ones who would never admit that girls talk about blow jobs in class. Those teachers are the ones in newspapers who run off with sixteen-year-olds to Florida.

And the talk. Naughty. I will always remember the girl (I say "girl," but she might have been twenty-five) who talked on her cell phone loudly and clearly about how much guys like it when girls rubbed their assholes while fucking. I knew demanding that she stop would be a futile effort and could possibly get me in trouble. The week before, a heroic sub at Washington Irving High School was pushed down a flight of stairs while strapped to a soda machine as if it were a sled. A couple of weeks before that, at a school in Harlem, a substitute teacher's hair was set ablaze by students. Reluctant to meet a similar fate, I merely let the student continue her naughty talk and tried to block it out until she asked me, "Don't men like it when you rub their anus?" Thank God, the bell rang just then.

I was thirty-seven when I started subbing in high schools in East Hampton. Juxtaposed with all that youth and testosterone made me feel so old and stupid. Undoubtedly UNcool. I remember once walking by some fresh-faced punks hanging out by their lockers and hearing one kid say to another, "Look at his pants" (mine). Together they laughed. Pushing forty, I do not mind it so much. I am old. I was cool once, sort of, and now I am not. I see it. I get it. Ultimately, I am okay with it. Anyway, God bless good teachers. I was not one.

AT LEAST I'M FUNNY: CONFESSIONS OF A HACK COMIC, THE ANATOMY OF A THIEF

I was a funny kid. As a dyslexic, I used outrageous humor as a coping technique. I was highly verbal and could lay down a story with the best of them. As I've said, at AA meetings I began to get laughs with my honest sharing from the floor. It was extremely validating. As with drugs, I wanted more. Around this time I took a Dale Carnegie public speaking class and won a competition by telling how I accidentally sank my stepfather's yacht.

I got the public speaking bug. I knew then that I wanted much more. I wanted to be a stand-up comedian.

I wanted to be a comedian to validate that I was alive; and have clout and power. After all, how could I be a fuckup loser if I got on *The Tonight Show*? (Never happened.) Let me first say that there might not be a better thrill in the world than writing a bit and then getting up onstage and telling it to a live audience. Aside from being a rock star (which must trump everything), there is no high like it. Even with all the glory there is in acting, getting new jokes that you wrote to work in front of strangers must beat being an actor. In *my* opinion. It is also probably the worst thing that can happen to a new comic because he is now hooked. The sky is the limit and he wants the sky and the sky is not in little comedy clubs, it is in TV and film. It is megastardom and the power that comes with it. Very few comics enjoy doing comedy for comedy's sake. We all want to be Mr. Big. We are using the stand-up venue as a vehicle to bigger things. That's what we are all after. Unfortunately, like people who buy lottery tickets, most of us fall short, and how could we not? There are very few megastars out there. In general, stand-up comics are neurotic, measurably self-absorbed people. A bad lot, all in all. With that said, it is fun getting a joke to work, and the love you get from the audience is so powerful it is addicting. Chasing that approval high, in my case, made me do some very unscrupulous things: namely steal other people's material.

A comedian admitting that he steals material is not unlike famous baseball players admitting they do steroids: a lot of them do it, but few, if any, will cop to it. I call these people pussies.

Even some of the most beloved names in comedy—Denis Leary, Robin Williams, and today's stars, like Jay Mohr, and, finally, the comic sensation women are literally throwing underwear at as if he were Elvis, Dane Cook—have faced controversy regarding claims of derivative and stolen material. Unlike the Barry Bonds situation, however, most people (except, of course, the comic whose material was lifted) don't seem to mind, including club owners.

To expose the underbelly of the comedy world, here is my story.

I constantly stole material and it had begun to wear me down. It had no longer been a means to an end; it was the end. I was faced with the age-old question many comics come to: was I stealing jokes to supplement my act, or had stolen jokes become my act?

There are literally thousands of working stand-up comedians in the USA today, and many of them steal or, more euphemistically, "lift" bits from fellow comics; it is a widespread problem affecting the entire industry, from amateurs to celebrities. You may rightfully say with contempt, "How could they?"

I hope that telling my story will shed some light on theft in the comedy world. Today New York City is witnessing a resurgence of stand-up comedy; there are more comedy clubs than ever. Perhaps this will serve as a guide to the customer, helping you to identify unoriginal, derivative, or "hack" material.

For a while it looked like I was on the road (pardon the pun) to becoming a legitimate stand-up comedian. Though I never got a spot on a major TV show like *Letterman* or *The Tonight Show* (sadly, the only real measuring stick of success for a comedian these days), I did open for established headliners like Lewis Black, Pat Cooper, and Robert Klein. I also performed at more than a hundred colleges over the years as a host of a game show called *Laugh, You Lose*. (Picture the worst episode of *The Price Is Right* and mix it with *The Gong Show* and *F-Troop*.) In New York City I was regular MC at Stand-Up NY, where I introduced acts such as Chris Rock and Robin Williams when they were in town to work on stuff. More important, I was starting to get respect (I like to think) inside my peer group. I mention this not to brag—believe me, I'm not proud; I was a B-level act at best—but to substantiate and qualify my experience. Actually, I was bad enough at stand-up that the label "hack comic" didn't apply in my case. I wish I could have been a hack; most hacks do well. But I was far too uncomfortable onstage, and my delivery was too rough to be a functioning hack comic.

But a thief! Yes, a thief—I was a natural. Stealing material (or bits), as mentioned, is epidemic in the comedy world, contaminating all levels; nearly all comics (probably 100 percent on cruise ships and at colleges where there is little surveillance/accountability) have lifted bits at some point. (There are exceptions to this: ethical guys who take pride in their work like Seinfeld and Dave Attell (possibly the most prolific and ingenious comic of all time), or lesser-known comic geniuses like Todd Barry and Jim Gaffigan, or even a Jim Norton, or my friend Russ Meneve, or Dan Naturman (all top NYC acts and names to look for). It is said that feelings of inadequacy drive us to steal. I would drop the "feelings" part and simply say that "inadequacy" drives us to steal. We are all great justifiers: "Well, it fits into my act," a comic might say, or it "augmented" or "supplemented" my already strong act.

I always respected the comedian who would stand in the raw wind and speak candidly about his or her thievery. Most comics, even when caught in the act, will go to the grave denying that they were indeed filthy thieves. (For comics, I've developed an exercise that might be able to cure you! Repeat after me: "I stole jokes because the jokes that I stole were better" (very good; keep going) "than the ones I wrote." Doesn't that feel better? It's emancipating, yes? Look, the reason I turned my head during math class in the seventh grade and looked at the girl's paper next to me was because she had a *better answer* than I did. It was that simple. When people ask me with condemnation: "How could you steal on the road?" My answer would be: How could you not steal on the road? It was like taking a test with no proctor and having the answer sheet.

I am sure a therapist could point to many different psychological reasons why I stole. But, again, I like to simplify it by saying this: the jokes that I stole simply worked better (got bigger laughs) than the ones I wrote myself. It is that simple.

There are probably many other reasons why I failed as a stand-up, chief among them, I imagine, being the fact that I was not necessarily all that exceptionally funny. (Clever, witty, yes;

hit-them-in-the-gut funny, no.) Other drawbacks included an annoying case of mental illness (OCD / paranoia / fear of New Balance sneakers, etc.) that manifested itself in bizarre preshow behavior, my inability to enunciate (slurred, garbled, guttural speech, stammering), and, though I had my moments, not being all that comfortable onstage. All this certainly hampered my success, but I would submit that what finally drove a stake through my stand-up career was my distorted sense of entitlement—or simply put, my inability to stop stealing material.

Sadly, many comics today fall into the traps and pitfalls of trying to "crowd please." Unlike other theatrical audiences, stand-up patrons are often distracted, rowdy, and participatory (not to mention hostile). A lot of times they are not interested in the little "routine" you wrote on the crosstown bus on the way to the club. So, what do you do when the crowd is not digging your stuff (not laughing)? You can: a) take the hit and bomb. Not really an option. The booker will say "Don't worry" and then never call you again. Or you can: b) revert to shticky sophomoric crowd work, like when a guy gets up to go to the bathroom, cup the mike, and in a deep announcerlike voice say: "Will all men with small penises please leave the room." (You say not funny? Guess again; the audience will howl at that, especially if the guy looks pissed off.) Or you can: c) flat out steal material.

I gave up comedy after doing a show at Catch a Rising Star in Princeton, New Jersey (should be renamed Catch a No-Name Hack). One show in particular really enlightened me as to how derivative and propped up my act had become. It was a Saturday night with a packed house, and they were ready to laugh. (If you can't kill on a Saturday night, you should get out of the business.) I did a lot of "stock stuff" up front, asking them if anyone was actually from Princeton at the club, knowing full well that no one was. There never is at that place, nor are there Princeton students; let's face it, comedy is by and large a pedestrian sport. When no one raised their hand, I hit them with the old "Good, then we can talk about the motherfuckers!" (Huge laugh.) Even if someone did raise their hand, I was safe because I could have said something like, "Good, can you give me a ride to the train station?" (A good hack always has an escape route.) After some more obligatory crowd work, as I wrote earlier, I started in with a *stolen* Jay Mohr bit I always used about how when a girl throws up after drinking too much she has ten friends helping hold her hair back. I did that bit for about two minutes. And by the way, when I say stolen, I am not fucking around here, I mean word for fucking word, not changing around some words and claiming it was mine like a lot of comics do today. I am talking about stealing the bit flat out.

So then, after Jay's bit (which got an applause break—thanks, Jay), I hit them with an old comic gimmick of pumping the mike stand and pretending that it was a keg and the microphone cord was the tap. (They loved it.) Then I went on to do a couple of "joke jokes"; probably the old "two women in supermarket dirty ball joke"—always a crowd favorite. (But any water fountain joke would work. Two Jews walk into a bar . . .) The place roared. Feeling buoyed by the energetic house that Saturday night, I thought to myself, *What the hell, these people will laugh at anything,* so I decided to throw in one of my own original jokes for good measure.

I laid out one of my bits about taking a career aptitude test and the results indicating that I would make an "outstanding hunter-gatherer." Suffice to say, it was like hitting a brick wall. The audience reacted as if it had been feasting on wonderful sweet strawberries and just accidentally bit into a rotten piece of Spam. The show came to a screeching halt (by the by, if you say "screeching halt" in your act, you are probably a hack). My act had taken a severe blow to starboard and was listing. I had to resuscitate the now stoned crowd, and to do this I returned to nuts and bolts, meat-and-potato hack crowd work. I simply pointed to a guy in the front row and asked if that was his wife sitting next to him. On cue, he looked at her (they always do), and then I said, "You have to look?" It always works. The crowd was back roaring. I closed with another Jay Mohr bit about sharing the soap in the shower. (Sorry, Jay.)

That night I came to the realization I had become essentially a "cover comic." Like a good wedding band or bar singer, I covered the classics. Sure, there was a light sprinkling of my own stuff in the act, but by stealing I was covering the greats. After all, when you go to a wedding, do you want to hear the band play the original crap they came up with in their garage the week before or bang out the standard Buddy Holly, Supremes, or Temptations? Who are we to deprive the audience of the classics—Murphy, Williams, Cosby? When I used to hire new acts for my low-end college game *Laugh, You Lose*, I used to beg them to steal, claiming "Why re-create the wheel? There is plenty of stuff already out there!" And I wonder why I got a bad reputation.

Stealing material is bad on so many levels it's tough to mention them all. The obvious ones are: bad reputation in the industry, low self-esteem associated with stealing, bad karma, and failure to develop original stuff.

I didn't start out as a thief. Actually, I was one of those guys you would see frantically scribbling ideas on yellow legal pads on the bus, subway, or park bench. I would bounce premises off anyone I met. I immersed myself in the open-mike circuit. All my time was spent with comics in diners or on the phone developing bits. I took workshops and comedy classes at NYU. I constantly had my hand inside one of those yellow Gotham City bins with "comedy workshop" boldly printed on them that used to clutter Manhattan sidewalks.

Ironically, I always got accolades on how original my stuff was. I believed (and still do) that I had a point of view and the persona and delivery to carry it out. Perhaps if I had stayed in NYC things would have ended up differently. I was quick to find out that on the road (where comics get paid real money) the audience was not into my pithy, wired, neurotic subjective humor. In Biloxi, Mississippi, they want to laugh and they want to laugh hard. And if you can't do the job, there are thousands of comics that can.

After only a few short weeks on the road, I realized that other people's bits seemed to work better than mine. Remember that joke of mine? "My SATs were so low that my entire school district lost funding." Not bad. But "Jammin' Jim" Florentine had a joke that went: "I loved the SAT. I did great on that test; it was the only test I ever got a one hundred on!" Now my joke had its qualities, but it lacked the pedestrian appeal of Jammin' Jim's joke. So I started to use his bit rather than my own.

Among comics there is an unspoken rule: what is said in Plattsburgh stays in Plattsburgh. Whatever you do, don't get caught stealing in Manhattan. I did, twice. The first time it was at a prom show at Stand-Up NY. The kids were digging me, so I let loose Jammin' Jim's SAT bit. The young crowed loved it. I got off stage and looked at the list of comics to follow me, and three comics down was Jammin' Jim. Holy shit! What to do? Should I be a man and approach Jim and tell him what I had done, saving him embarrassment and rage? Or, since I had not heard him do comedy for a few years, should I hope that he developed new material and didn't do the SAT anymore? Avoiding confrontation has always been a character defect of mine. So I let Jammin' Jim take the stage and kept my fingers crossed. It was his second joke. Not only did the audience not laugh, but they booed him. I ran out of the club as Jim was questioning the audience why they didn't like the bit. The audience was more than willing to furnish him with an answer. "Because the guy that stutters just told it!" I might add that I just saw Larry the Cable Guy do a joke that Jammin' Jim did ten years ago. "A cop pulled me over and asked if I had been drinking. I asked the cop: do you see a fat girl in the seat next to me?" Now, who wrote that joke?

I wrote an article in *Penthouse* about joke theft. Howard Stern read it and had me call in to talk about it on his show. I thought I could take this subject and run with it, but on the show I tightened up like the Holland Tunnel at rush hour. It did not go well, and Howard rushed me off the air. I don't blame him; I was a stuttering maniac. But we missed out on a good thing, kind of a whose-joke-was-it bit.

I had clever enough stuff, but, as Dave Attell (host of Comedy Central's *Insomniac* and hands down the most prolific comic working today), says, "Write all the jokes you want, but there is nothing funnier than a fat guy falling off a Jet Ski."

The reason I did Attell's eggnog bit (Do you know what eggnog is? Elf cum.) in Florida was that it was better than anything I wrote, not because it fit, or a lady had a drink that looked like eggnog, or it "just came out as I was improvising." (That's the best one: it "just came out," as Robin Williams once put it. Thanks for paving the way, Robin.) I saw Attell at Stand-Up NY and I went up to him and said, "Do you know I did your eggnog joke down in Florida and it bombed?" Feeling completely unthreatened by me (Dave knows a broken man when he sees one), he replied, "I know; sometimes that one can be tricky." Fact is, if the audience doesn't dig you, it doesn't matter whose stuff you're stealing, you are going nowhere in this business. Dave knew this.

While my bits weren't great, at least I wasn't talking about the movie *Indecent Exposure*, or John Bobbitt (had penis cut off by wife) or Joey Buttafuoco or Michael Jackson's white-glove stuff or the lady who poured steaming hot coffee on her pussy and sued McDonald's for five million (actually, that was pretty funny). My point is that I was not like a lot of new comics who decide they want to be a comic, walk into a comedy club, hear what other comics are talking about, then rearrange some words and claim it as their own.

There are a million comics out there, half of them with derivative bits using buzzwords like *restraining order* or *stalking* or *press charges* (as in I hope she doesn't). If my material had a flaw, it was too subjective (i.e., Richard Lewis talking about how neurotic he is) rather than objective (Jerry Seinfeld talking about airplane travel). Generally speaking, audiences at the clubs want objective humor (lost socks in a dryer). Some subjective comics like the late great self-deprecating king Rodney Dangerfield break through ("The first time I had sex, I was very scared . . . I was all alone"). No one made fun of himself like Dangerfield; I tried, but I did not have his incredible stage presence: sweating like a pig, those big bulging bug eyes, his twitchy persona. What a character; what a franchise! (Shut your eyes and picture a giant balloon doll of Rodney in the Macy's Thanksging Day parade.)

Dangerfield was an exception and a phenomenon, but for the most part, people in comedy clubs generally want to hear about their own worlds: their roads, their food, their cars, their husbands or wives. They want to point at their spouse and say, "You do that with the toothpaste (or the TV clicker)!" I was quick to find out that audiences were not into some dude talking about how his hygiene was so poor that, "if he had a vagina it would certainly stink . . ." (My own bit, thank you very much!) I did have some clean stuff: "A lot of guys are looking for a girl who wants to settle down. I am looking for a girl who simply wants to settle." It was okay, but it did not get the belly laugh I needed to make money in comedy.

I started in 1995, probably the worst time in comedy history to start a career. It was the very end of the comedy boom. As with disco in the '80s, America had had enough of stand-ups. There was simply too much of it on TV. Even Hollywood, after years of plucking talent from comedy clubs (Tim Allen, Ray Romano, Drew Carey, Roseanne, Rosie O'Donnell), lost interest. Comedy was out, karaoke was in; reality TV was on the horizon.

Because the comedy clubs were now empty, it was up to the new comics to supply their own audience. I had all the symptoms of a beginning New York comic. For one, I had no more friends left. You begin to see your old friends less as friends and more as potential audience members, or, better put, asses in the seats. First, you blaze through your college and work friends, then you go through all your high school friends, then one day you find yourself riffling through your old grammar school yearbooks: "Hello, Pete. Hi, this is Jeff Nichols. I used to sit next to you in the third grade. Look, I'm doing stand-up now and I was wondering if you were doing anything Monday night around seven?"

Once you run out of friends and family members, you constantly look to new pools of humans to find support. To reach my prescribed quota of audience members, I would go to AA meetings and prey upon unsuspecting newcomers. "Hi, congratulations on one week sober. . . . Hey, by the way, here's a flyer; why don't you come to a bar and hear me talk about how my orgasms have the consistency of skim milk?"

I used to bribe bookers and agents with cosmetics (my stepfather was in the business and could get me samples), Broadway theater tickets, even cash, which got me a lot of stage time early on. (They all went down, by the way, with the exception of the late Lucien Hold, the infamous booker of the World Famous Comic Strip. God bless him, he would take the stuff and still not give me stage time.)

Two years into stand-up I was getting half-hour feature gigs in places like Myrtle Beach, South Carolina; Lancaster, Pennsylvania, Tampa, Florida. Actually, I didn't start stealing until about a year later. Like a lot of us, I used to justify my thievery by using joke-jokes, or "stock material," a euphemism for gags so commonly used they had become generic. (Face it, "two Jews walk into a bar with a parrot," is stealing, too, if you didn't write it originally . . . you filthy hack), or by claiming that I was simply "augmenting" or "supplementing" my act to fill up time.

My thievery took root after an agent got me a gig in Ocean

City, Maryland, a busy resort community. I had to pull a half hour, two shows a night for two weeks. At the time, I did not know about stock humor, or joke-jokes; I didn't even think about stealing. The first show didn't go so well, but the second one was a blast. My stuff worked, I got applause breaks! I got paid for it! Holy shit, I was a comic! I remember running around the complex outside, jumping up and down like a mental patient. I had arrived! I was a professional! It was like scoring a goal in a lacrosse game, as good as getting laid.

But for the next ten shows I struggled. It was then that the booker called and told me that I should add some stock joke-jokes to my act. He even suggested a well-known joke book. The next night I did (I don't remember all of the jokes, but I think one had the words *moose cock* in it); they worked and it was all downhill from there. The war was over and I had lost.

Even an elite act can fall prey. Five years ago I was in the back of Stand-Up NY and there was a huge act there, a world-famous mega movie star onstage really hacking it up. I think he had ten minutes of Viagra jokes and another ten on Bobbitt. In between he was doing all stock crap. Now, here I was, a broke, struggling, remarkably unsuccessful comic, but somehow despite the fame and wealth that this guy had acquired I felt bad for him. He looked tired and diminished as if he were suffering from low self-esteem. The audience was digging him, but not as much as when he first got up onstage. At first the crowd was starstruck, but now he was waning a bit. He didn't have the glow of an open-miker who had just made a new bit work! He was not benefiting from the therapeutic value of original comedy, the stuff that makes guys like Carlin and Seinfeld get back onstage year after year. He was not engaging or challenging the crowd intellectually like Lenny Bruce or Chris Rock. He was smoke and mirrors; he was, dare I say, a hack. Soon after that, Williams was caught on David Letterman's show completely stealing a bit that Ray Romano had been doing for ten years.

Then there was this cat on *The Tonight Show* a while back, a dude named Dane Cook. He was animated, cool, and likable, though, God bless him, he had clear shades of Brian Regan (not really his fault; we all can't be Todd Barry or Attell). Anyway, he was doing a bit about freaky people in the workplace, the obligatory pens jammed in the pocket stuff, not all that original, but I was going along with it. He seemed to be having fun, plus he was cute, and like many managers today, I like a cute act. But then he mentioned a character who had "that stomach under the belt thing going." Now, yes, it's a gray area and, yes, the dude could have come up with it on his own. But, for three years I had heard Patrick O'Neal talk about the same stomach under the belt. So I looked into it and I'm not the only one who thinks he's a thief.

One time I was up in Toronto performing at a place called The Comedy Wood, where they insisted that the feature pull thirty minutes (some places will let you get by with twenty-five, even twenty). I had about ten solid minutes of clever, if not necessarily all that funny material. So what to do? Well, first I started the show with a thinly veiled variation of Brian Regan's famous "You, too" bit. I thought I neatly couched it by putting the scene in a Canadian airport. After checking my passport, the customs people say, "Enjoy your trip to Canada," and I nervously respond, "You, too!" The worst part of this was that the managers of the club loved the bit, and when I left and arrived at the club, they would say: "You, too!" to me. Can you imagine the shame? (I should have made up "You, too!" T-shirts and sold them.)

Sadly, what I once thought was a decent act coupled with a merging persona had degenerated into derivative, stolen garbage. One time onstage I had a brain fart and started to tell a stolen bit that I had already done a few minutes before. Halfway through it, I realized it and asked the crowd "Did I already do this?" When they collectively yelled "Yes!" I said, "What's funny about that is not that I did the same joke twice, but that it was not my joke to begin with." No one laughed except for a fellow comic, Pete Correale, who fell off his stool howling in the back of the club.

As if stealing jokes was not enough, I also found myself starting to lift entire personas. A lot of guys do this, but my problem was that I could not seem to stick to one persona. I found myself vacillating and drifting, rudderless, in the middle of huge, abrupt, and conspicuous persona swings. One moment, I would be cupping the mike and talking calmly like the great Todd Barry and next moment I'd be screaming like a mental patient, i.e., Joey Cola. I can't imagine what those persona shifts looked like to the audience.

But the stolen bit I'm most ashamed of rightfully belonged to comedian Stephanie Bloom, which brings me to the other time I was caught stealing stuff in New York. Stephanie was an open miker/schoolteacher performing at Stand-Up NY's funniest teacher contest. I had won the contest the year before and had a guest spot on the show. Stephanie was buoyant and confident, and she laid out a great bit, I thought: "The games the kids play today have all changed since we were kids. We used to play red light, green light; today they play freeze, motherfucker!" I went up to Stephanie after the show and genuinely complimented her and encouraged her to keep performing.

Later I was at the Funny Bone in Pittsburgh and had the place rolling with my own inner-city teaching stuff, but I felt that I had to take them to another level; I wanted more! So Stephanie's joke simply rolled off my tongue almost like it was meant to be. I didn't care at the time. *Who was Stephanie Bloom anyway?* I thought to myself that I was meant to hear that joke that night so I could appropriate it. I was an act, goddamnit it! She probably had stopped doing comedy by that point anyhow.

I was very wrong; Stephanie was doing just fine and gaining the respect of her peers. I did her joke at a Caroline's taping and the comic Eddie Brill called me out on it. I was caught like a rat.

My reputation sucked, I caught shit wherever I went. It was actually fun sometimes—I loved telling comics who called me a thief that they need not worry, their stuff was safe. But like a quarterback in the grasp of a linebacker, it was time to take a knee.

The final nail in the coffin was when I overheard an audience member tell his friend that I made him uncomfortable and that he found me disturbing. I had overheard people say I was not funny, that I sucked, but never had I heard I was "disturbing." "Disturbing" is the polar opposite of "funny" and not what a comic should be. It was time to get out.

THE FREAK SHOW

Before I gave up stand-up comedy completely, as I mentioned, a low-life agent coaxed me into hosting a game show at community colleges across the country. He made it sound good by saying that I would be playing at major universities, traveling to various cities, and making some nice money! The show was entitled *Laugh, You Lose* and was a spinoff of an old vaudeville show called *Make Me Laugh*, in which the contestant would sit in a chair and the comic would try to make him or her laugh. If the comic failed, the contestant would get a turn at spinning the prize wheel and winning cash.

My job was to assemble a few comics, pack them into a van, and tour around the country, playing at mostly community and state colleges. I first hired traditional comics, set-up-punch-line guys regarded as "established comics" and with real television credits. (Some comics I had in that van went on to success in Hollywood: John Viener is one of the head writers and characters on ABC's *Family Guy*; Brody Stevens is on a sports TV show; Dan Naturman and Russ Meneve are among the top comics in the country today. With the exception of Comedy Central's Asian wonder Steve Byrne, all these comics sucked on my show. They were great performers elsewhere, but not on my show. Where is Chris Farley when you need him! The problem was that if the students did not laugh (they never did), the prize money would come out of my pocket. Sometimes a student spun the "cash wheel" to win three hundred dollars. On top of this expense, I had to pay the comics, get hotel rooms, and pay for gas. Again, the comics that I first brought out simply could not execute in that environment.

My first semester I grossed a hundred grand but had to put it all back into the show. I was hemorrhaging so much money that I was reduced to gambling with the students. When a kid once won a couple hundred bucks off me, I told him that I would bet him double or nothing on a fifty-fifty bet. He went for it. I had him flip a quarter. He called heads. He won. I gave him a hundred bucks to pacify him and then took his address and shamelessly informed him that the "agency" would be sending him a check in a week or two. I then took off knowing full well that the student would not receive the money. Other times I told students that I would "have to go to the cash machine," then pile the guys in the van and bolt. A few times we had enraged kids chase the van as we pulled away.

When I returned to the city, I decided that using traditional comics was not the way to go. I saw the success that Howard Stern was having with his freak show format, and thought that if I rounded up some interesting characters the show might work. It took some doing, but eventually I had a gorgeous mosaic of characters. The show became a politically incorrect "shock" show. I had a drag queen, a dwarf, a possibly mentally ill Chinese man who sang show tunes (though probably not since I think the Chinese usually hide their mentally ill), and a fat guy. I figured I would have no problem with the fat guy because he looked like a giant lesbian, but he got off to a bad start because he chose to do political jokes and failed miserably. It was not until I demanded that he put on a giant diaper and do jumping jacks in front of the contestant that his act took off. Look, I don't make the rules: fat is funny.

At one point, one of my acts quit, so I hired a fifty-five-year-old prostitute to come along with us. I thought she would be

great. My plan was for her to go onstage drunk and give elaborate reasons why she could "suck the contestant's cock better
than any cheerleader on campus." The audience would certainly
break out into hysterical laughter, I thought. This never came
to pass, though. She did not want to leave Huntsville, Alabama,
for only one hundred bucks a show. (The ego!) Sometimes the
shows were so good that we got standing ovations. I was netting
a thousand a show. Other times the shows did not go so well,
particularly if the school's entrance had a huge cross with Jesus
nailed to it. Sometimes the college administration complained,
as in the following:

MSOE MILWAUKEE SCHOOL OF ENGINEERING   1025 N. Broadway   Milwaukee, WI 53202-3109   414-277-7300 http://www.msoe.edu/

December 11, 1997

Kramer International, Inc.
Attn: Robert Kramer
3849 Lake Michigan Drive
Grand Rapids, Michigan 49544

Dear Mr. Kramer:

Per our telephone conversation of 12-11-97, I am providing the following information regarding the performance of the "You Laugh, You Lose" Comedy Show that took place at our campus last evening (Wednesday, 12-10-97). First of all, we were extremely disappointed and offended to say the least with the quality, content and character of the actual performance. Your advertisements as listed in the NACA Programming Magazine make claim that the show is "100% Clean". How we realize that such a claim can be interpreted differently, but I find that there is no other way to interpret the show last evening except to refer to it as "totally offensive, inappropriate, crass, rude, and vulgar".

So that you know exactly what I am referring to, I will repeat, as best I can recall, just some of the jokes or comments that were made by the "comedians". Here they are: 1) sticking a hand in his pants, through the zipper, and saying, "hi I am John Hancock", 2) saying "you are the load your mother should have swallowed"; 3) talking about being "hung like a moose" and saying things about underwear; 4) saying "I am going to fuck you up the ass"; 5) fake punching in the face, stomach, and the crotch area of a contestant; 6) saying "tell me where your father touched you, show me on the doll"; 7) referring to their own genitals and saying "I am going to whip it out"; 8) numerous comments about masturbation; 9) asking audience members if they are "fags" or "lesbians"; and 10) sticking their butts in the contestant faces, referring to being "someone's bitch" in prison and making other crude comments. Now these are just a few of the comments that were made. Finally, the game show seemed to evolve into a simple acts of money distribution to get the show over with, asking contestants to "spin the wheel" and guess if the number will be odd or even for $10 dollars.

In hindsight, it is a regret that we did not stop the show and ask the comedians to pack up. It has been suggested by members of our administration to not have a Kramer Agency act on campus again. This would consist of ending the current contractual agreement and take the financial loss on our end or having your agency, in good faith, release us from the agreement. Unfortunately we have already sent the payment for the comedy act in advance of the performance, so we are unable to withhold payment. I am confident that your agency did not win "NACA Agency of the Year" by providing such acts to college campuses and we will reflect such a concern in the NACA performance review of this comedy show. On behalf of the students at the Milwaukee School of Engineering, we look forward to your response. I may be reached at (414) 277-7225 or (414) 277-6922.

Sincerely,

Richard Gagliano
Student Center Program Coordinator

c. Patrick Coffey, Dean of Students
  Alan Hoesly, Director of Student Activities

Yes, yes, I realize that the letter is unreadable as reproduced, and since we can't enlarge it in its original form, I will re-create it here. The letter, dated December 11, 1997, is from the student center coordinator at the Milwaukee School of Engineering, where we performed, to my booker, Kramer International, Inc.:

Dear Mr. Kramer,

Per our telephone conversation of 12-11-97, I am providing the following information regarding the performance of the "Laugh, You Lose" comedy show that took place on our campus last evening (Wednesday 12-10-97). First of all, we are extremely disappointed and offended to say the least with the quality, content, and character of the actual performance. Your advertisement as listed in the NCAA programming magazine made claim that the show is "100% clean". Now we realize that such a claim can be interpreted differently, but I find that there is no other way to interpret the show last evening except to refer to it as totally offensive, inappropriate, crass, rude and vulgar.

So that you know exactly what I am referring to, I will repeat, as best I can remember, just some of the jokes or comments that were made by the "comedians." Here they are: 1) Sticking a hand in his pants, through the zipper, and saying "Hi I am John Handcock"! 2) Saying "you are the load your mother should have swallowed". 3) talking about being "hung like a moose" and saying things about moosecock. 4) Saying "I am going to fuck you up the ass" 5) Fake punching in the face, stomach, and the crotch, area of the contestant. 6) Saying, "Tell me where your father touched you, show me on the doll". 7) Referring to their own genitals and saying: "I am going to whip it out" 8) numerous comments about masturbation. 9) Asking audience *members if they are fags and lesbians and 10) sticking their butts in the contestants' faces, referring to being someone's bitch in prison and making other crude comments. Now, these are just a few of the comments that were made. Finally the "game show" seemed to evolve into simple acts of money distribution to get the show over with; asking contestants to "spin the wheel" and guess if the number will be odd or even for $10 dollars.*

In hindsight, it is a regret that we did not stop the show and ask the comedians to pack it up. It has been suggested by a member of our staff not to have a Kramer Agency show on our campus again. This would consist of ending our current contract agreement. . . . I am confident that your agency did not win "NACA agency of the year" by providing such acts to campuses and we will reflect this in the NCAA performance review of this comedy show.

Again, just as with Nichols Enterprises, I was ill equipped to run my own business. I kept no receipts, no records of whom and when I paid. I was a mess. While I had some good ideas on how the show could work, I ultimately drove it into the ground. I remember one of the last shows, in Bridgeport, Connecticut. I was taking an ice cube and squeezing it out of my hand and saying to the audience and contestant, "This is my impression of an Eskimo peeing," and watching the ice cube fall to the floor. It really was time to get out and move on.

When you first start doing stand-up comedy a lot of the open mics are in the late afternoon/early evening (4 p.m. to 7 p.m.). Most comics hated open mics but I kind of liked them. It gave me some structure and I liked the people. I had just finished with one of my two sets when a particularly shady comic that I knew came up to me and asked me if I wanted to go to a really nasty strip club across town—it was around 5 p.m. on a Monday, my response was immediate: "Yes . . . Yes I would!"

The place was very close to Wall Street. When you walked in the door you knew instantly that it was a dump; there was the obligatory indifferent fat guy at the door collecting five-dollar entry fees and the place did not have the sanitary night club atmosphere of say Scores or Flash Dancers, two notorious strip clubs in New York City.

Upon walking upstairs, I was quick to notice that this was more of a dungeon (literally) than a strip club. There were no tables or chairs, just a bunch of haggard-looking couches alone in a room. Now I know everything in life is subjective, but when I say there was not an attractive stripper there, you have to take my word for it; it was a filthy scene indeed. The first thing I noticed was that there were no poles and no girls were stripping or dancing. The only thing that was going on was dry humping, lots of dry humping (specifically, middle-aged topless women straddling men and gyrating as hard as they could on top of the men's crotches). The second thing that really stood out with me is that the majority of the guys had sweat pants on. I remember registering this as odd.

So my friend disappears somewhere into this hell hole, and I find a seat next to two guys who were in the middle of getting dry-humped. (My guess is that it was one dry hump per song.) Now, I had fair warning: I knew that the selection of strippers was not going to be hot young debutantes; on the way over, my comic friend told me that one of them actually had a bullet wound across her stomach. Still, I was not prepared for the fact that the strippers appeared to be much older than me (at the time I was twenty-eight or so) and I am sure this comes across as incredibly racist but many reminded me of cleaning ladies that used to work for my mother. Some had to be in their fifties. The crazy part of all this was it was tough to get ahold of one of the "dancers."

The place was mobbed. I know one may wonder why I did not leave, but the saying goes "when in Rome. . . ." I finally grabbed one of the ladies' attention walking by between songs. She was a Hispanic woman and really did not have anything sexy about her save possibly for her outfit, probably a negligee of some sort. Anyway, you think she would be a little more pleasant to compensate for the other inadequacies, specifically (considering her profession) her weathered looks. But this woman was nothing short of hostile. "Fifteen dollars for a dance."

Now this was the early nineties and twenty bucks a dance was what they got at high-end strip clubs (I was told), so this price seemed a bit high. Anyway, this women sat on top of me and basically beat my balls in with her ass for about three minutes or however long the song played. The first two songs I didn't even have a hard-on, but as the woman grinded away on me, I realized why all the guys had sweat pants on; the idea was to have an orgasm in your pants, to be dry-humped to the point of climax.

So now I was about sixty bucks in the hole, and goddamn it I was going to cum no matter how much my balls hurt. I asked for one more dance, and as this angry, saggy-breasted, middle-aged, probably mother of four, Hispanic woman crashed down on my groin with remarkable fury, I remember trying to think of any other erotic sexual experience I had had in the past, my mind rifled through an array of encounters. With all the friction and with barely a sliver of a hard-on, I came. I remember my penis was pointed down to my leg so my orgasm shot directly down my pants. The woman could tell something had happened and stopped dry-humping me right away. Looking back, she asked sternly, "No more?" I said, "No more, thanks." And she got up and walked away without a word.

As I stood up to go, I realized another reason why all the guys were wearing sweats: I had cum streaming down my leg into my sock. I pigeon-toed it to the bathroom in search of a paper towel or at least some toilet paper, but no such luck there. I staggered out into the sunlight. It was a summer evening around 6 p.m. and respectable people were getting out of work; I felt like a vampire thrown into the light. I had another comedy spot uptown at Stand-Up NY Comedy Club on the West Side at 7 p.m., so I staggered to a pay phone (early nineties pre-cell-phone era) and called the club and canceled my gig. My head lowered, I got on the number seven subway line for a long depressing pilgrimage back to Queens with shame running down my leg. I went home and stared at my wall all night.

TIME OUT: THE AFFAIR

I am told over and over again by awful Hollywood movies (including my own) that all stories need a love interest. So, here is what I got. By the time I was in my mid-thirties, my experience with sex was minimal, especially after I got sober. It has been basically confined to the occasional prostitute and pints of Häagen-Dazs. Even when I was doing comedy, women still fled from me. Perhaps it was the constant jabs in my act about my sagging nuts and premature ejaculation.

When drunk, as I've said, I got laid. God knows with what

or whom, but it happened. Sober, I faced a lifetime of celibacy, which is not without its own merits. The problem is that I live in a city that has beautiful women on every block. Lust rears its ugly head.

When I made the decision to go on antidepressants the doctor told me that the only negative side effect would be a lowered sex drive. I remember thinking this was not a side effect but an unexpected perk. I was so sexually frustrated at the time that I believe I would have volunteered to have my libido yanked out. Perhaps elective castration was in order. I would no longer gawk at women. In fact, I could walk by beautiful women with casual indifference.

Rarely invited to parties, tense from my massive caffeine intake, and no blue ribbon winner in the looks category, I was relegated to occasionally trolling AA meetings for women.

The AA waters are troubled indeed. While there are some wonderful women in the program, it is a virtual mine field of borderline psychotics, complete with eating disorders and body image problems.

Was meeting women the only reason I went to AA? I do not think so. At least I hope not. AA has provided me with insights both on a spiritual and practical level, but I did not think a little action on the side would be that bad.

So I met this woman. In the beginning she knew very little about me. It was pure lust and drama. Then, I guess she grew tired of my poor hygiene, premature ejaculation (look, when it begins to feel good I come; it's that simple), and the fact that she had to spend countless hours at night constantly trying to persuade me that I was not dying of MS and not a loser.

What began as lust had finally become a liability. Although

I am sure she liked me or at least had some compassion for me, she did not want to screw me anymore.

We met at a coffee shop, which is what you do in AA. You go to coffee shops after meetings. It is a validating experience and can be a lot of fun. The inherent problem with this and for any group outing in general is that the seating arrangements are far too random. I never seemed able to sit in the vicinity of desirable women. "Desirable" means not above sixty. It sounds awful. I love older people. I just prefer, if possible, not to fuck them. It always seemed that I wound up next to some male new-comer from Ozone Park, Queens, who worked for the transit department and happened to be "a little light" on cash. I am a wretched man indeed.

Lightning struck one night when I found myself sitting across from this beautiful girl. Look, I have been honest about everything in this book so far—you have to take my word on this: she was Kim Basinger beautiful. I had met her before and was privy to the fact that she had a boyfriend. Knowing she was completely out of my league took the pressure off and allowed me to be relaxed and uninhibited. We laughed for two hours. We even shared a cab home. When we reached her house, I really wanted to say something cool like, "By the way, if you ever break up with your boyfriend I would love to take you out." Instead, I blurted out that I thought I might have lupus.

She happened to be in show business, so I told her that I needed some help and gave her my number.

"I have a question for you. Would you be good enough to call me back?" she said in an answering machine message the next day. I had been in this position before. I figured she was going to ask me what all beautiful women ask me: would I like to go out with her fat, unattractive, and hostile girlfriend with nice eyes? Since I am a "nice guy" I am always set up with the homely friends. It is a crude truth, but, hey, I don't make the rules.

I called her back and five minutes into the conversation I realized that she really had no question for me at all. It was all small talk. She asked me if I was dating anyone and if I was going to a meeting that night. She suggested that we get some coffee afterward.

At this point I still did not think that she liked me biblically, but I got my little ass over to that meeting. After the meeting we walked down to SoHo where AA people tended to have coffee and gossip. Then she said she had coffee at her place and asked if I wanted to go there.

"Yes! Yes, I would!" I responded with no hesitation. I figured I was in the "friend realm," which was fine with me. It beat hanging out at the Papaya King by myself. I also assumed the boyfriend would be there too.

Her place was nothing short of palatial. It was a huge loft apartment with high ceilings, many rooms, and a huge open kitchen. Of course, the first thing I noticed was that the boyfriend was conspicuously absent. I innocently queried as to his whereabouts and she told me that he spent most of his time in Los Angeles.

We brewed coffee and watched television. I had mentioned a certain show that I like and it turned out she had some episodes on tape. She said we could watch it if I wanted. In the bedroom. I said I did.

I was surprised to find only a bed in the bedroom.

"Am I getting up on this?" I asked.

"Yes."

I jumped onto the bed enthusiastically. As hours went by we started getting cozy. I started to believe that I was dropping out of the friend realm (safe but boring) and into the potential lover role (unfamiliar and terrifying).

We watched several episodes and had to work through some awkward moments because we did not have the marvelous sexual tool, alcohol, at our disposal. Let's face it—alcohol can be a beautiful thing. If I had had my "sway on," I would have been trying to jam my tongue down the back of her throat inside of five minutes. As it was, I felt like Forrest Gump.

After about two hours of paralyzing indecision, dry mouth, and awkwardness, I realized that our feet were touching. Green light! But just like in the movie *Animal House*, I had the devil on one shoulder and an angel on the other.

"Hold off! You will meet an available girl. Wait. Do the right thing and your higher power will ante up some legitimate booty for you eventually," said the angel.

"Are you crazy? You have not gotten laid in five years! You are in no position to take the moral high ground here. Go ahead! Have some fun!" said the devil.

So I did it. It was immoral, dirty, and wonderfully erotic. Given that the rich boyfriend lived primarily in LA, I essentially moved in, sometimes for a week at a clip. I would substitute teach during the day and run home to her at night. When "Mr. Big" was in town, I would split and hang out at Barnes & Noble in a fit of jealousy. I was obsessed and impossible to be around.

When I slithered back over to the loft to screw her again, I was not only screwing her, I was screwing him and his money. (God, I wish I fucked better; I would have really given it to her.

Incidentally, I would love just once not to have to say the word "sorry" after I come.) I liked to demonize the guy, but I had to fight off the insidious thought that maybe he was really a good guy. And there I was walking around like a dog in his apartment, wearing his bathrobe.

What sucked most of all was that she had been through a lot in her life and went to AA to get better. I did not help matters. I tried to break it off a bunch of times, but she was too powerful. More accurately, the "vagina" was too powerful. In fact, it wins nine out of ten times.

I am not sure what she saw in me, other than that I was a nice guy. Perhaps she got off on watching a guy destroying himself. Other than that first night, I never recalled laughing with her again. (This might be because I was always distracted by the fact that her forehead did not move at all. It practically dripped Botox.)

As far as the sex went, I was so strung out on caffeine, nicotine, and antidepressants that my hard-ons were weak at best. One time when she was on top, I shit in the bed a little. I had had a lot of coffee and was very nervous. It was not a total blowout, which in hindsight would have been pretty funny, but just a little squirt. It was enough though that she pointed to the sheets and asked me, "What is that?"

Anyway, I loved going down on her, though I am not sure if I was good or not. For me it did not matter. It transcended sex. It was about comfort. I was so terrified of life that I sought refuge in her vagina. I felt as if I were trying to climb back into the safety of the womb.

To this day I do not think we shared the same interests or ideologies. Even if she did really like my personality, I cannot blame her for not leaving Mr. Big for me. I would not if I were in her shoes. I was not a successful person. What was she going to do? Leave him and move in with me at the local YMCA?

CATERING IN THE HAMPTONS

I was dead broke when a friend of mine, Jonathan, who ran a catering service, asked if was interested in working for him, catering at high-class parties in the Hamptons.

Sure, my first instinct was that—at the age of thirty-five, the age that one wakes up and screams, Holy shit, I am a colossal loser!, and since I'm supposedly in show business—I would rather go as a guest to the "high class" parties in the Hamptons, than schlep bus buckets for them. But the more I thought about it, the more I realized that I had been to a lot of parties in my life—in fact, I imagine I am a pretty good example of the proverbial "guy who stayed at the party too long." I hadn't been at a function in a long time and the one that I did attend, I believe I contaminated with negative energy. Ironically, if I may boast, I used to be the life of the party; granted they were not Hampton parties, but nevertheless I was a real conversationalist at those frat-house basement things. I was also wacked out on coke half the time.

The last party I went to, I suppose due to years of dropping acid at Grateful Dead shows, I was having problems simply staying in conversations. I found myself being offended by a seemingly banal question like, "So what do you do for a living?" How dare they! I found their line of questioning to be intrusive and invasive. I was reduced to standing in the corner and mutating.

(One guy simply asked me my name once, and I had to say Um, in front of it. Um, Jeff Nichols. Now, isn't your name, of all the words out there, something you should be able to summon without hesitation?) The more I thought about it, the more I realized that I probablywould be better off working at a party than I would be "mingling."

In addition, I have always subscribed to the theory that all jobs, with the exception of abducting newborns from hospitals (tough on self-esteem and stressful I imagine) have dignity. I had had enough of them, including substitute teaching, dictionary salesman, handing out flyers, ushering, et cetera, and I was not embarrassed at all to do the work. So I got to thinking more about it. With the exception of oppressed people, most of us have choices in our lives; for instance, while other kids were doing their homework, I chose to snort Wite-Out correction fluid (an office supply) to get high. Here is my point: some of us make choices that have us ending up at Hamptons parties, some of us make choices that, well, simply put, have us working at Hampton parties. I got very Zen about my insight. I was ready to shed my elitist attitude and "become a worker among workers." Even the very real possibility of running into an old girlfriend or employer did not faze me.

Being that I have no car (or health insurance for that matter), I had to be picked up. A superficial survey of my fellow caterers revealed a motley crew indeed. The catering service was named something light and cheery like "Red Rose Caterers." It would have been more accurately named "the needle and the damage done catering service."

They were nice guys though. Most, like me, were doing it for the first time. We were all quick to find out that catering is constant work. There are no scheduled breaks and while you may make 300 bucks catering, you may have to spend a thousand dollars the next day for an MRI of your lower lumbar. Lifting bus buckets is brutal on one's back.

The party was at a palatial mansion right on the beach. We spent a few hours in the hot sun setting up chairs, tables, and bars. Then I had four job assignments. The first job was to go around, in a traditional manner, handing out hors d'oeuvres. This entailed walking through the party while balancing a platter with some culinary offerings. I thought that I was doing all right; I mean I had a little problem with eye contact and all. (Are you supposed to look at people in the face or bow your head subserviently when presenting food?) And there was one awkward moment with a lady who was breast-feeding a baby (I may have leered), but all in all, I thought I was doing OK. Although, I must add that for whatever reason the other caterers all had the good stuff that the guests wanted, like the jumbo shrimp or the filet mignon; people flocked to their offerings. I apparently had the "experimental tray." I got saddled with cucumbers with salsa on the top; I might just as well have been walking around with sliced Spam.

So I was going about my business, when my friend Jonathan came over with a concerned look on his face. He told me that he was going to have to take me off the floor. When I asked why, he told me that he had gotten some complaints that I was making the guests uncomfortable. In addition he saw me eating. "Don't you know," he continued, "that caterers should always be smiling?" This pissed me off—what did he expect from a guy schlepping a tray of cucumbers at a party at the age of thirty-six? Did he want me to summon that "The-world-is-my-oyster-

and-I'm-in-love-with-Susie" grin that I had in high school? I had news for Jon: there had been a lot of water under the bridge since those days, my teeth were yellow, and I was not smiling. Perhaps he expected me to break out singing a show tune like "Hello Dolly." "Look," I curtly told him, "if I am catering at this party, I am one bad decision away from living in a trailer home. I am not smiling."

In retrospect, perhaps I did come across a little too pensive and nervous. I knew I did not look too good—gaunt from bad diet, cigarettes, and caffeine. Also, from snorting all that ecstasy in college, I have a slight problem with my equilibrium, causing me to sway some; perhaps I bumped into someone inadvertently.

For my next job, Jon assigned me to be a bartender. While I immediately told him I was not suited for such a position, he told me it would be no problem. People would primarily only ask for wine, beer, or soda, with the occasional gin and tonic. I was all right with that, until my first customer showed up, a beautiful, healthy, professional type, with an air of extreme self-confidence. She smiled widely exposing her white radiant teeth, the ocean majestically crashing behind her, and she happily asked me for a Cal 24. A Cal 24! What the fuck was that? To this day, I still don't know what it is, some kind of martini, I suppose. The most pathetic thing is that I began to make it; I filled up a big glass of ice, looked at her and told her I would be right back, then ran off to find another bartender.

I kept at it. I was thrown off a couple more times by requests for vodka gimlets, and cosmopolitans, but I gave it my all. When Jon came up to check on me, I was practically, once again, in the familiar fetal position. Red wine all over my shirt, with confused, annoyed guests wrestling over bottles in an attempt to make their own drinks.

Jon then ushered me off to my next job—as a clearer. My job was to do just that, clear the tables. He told me that I should be clearing at all times. I could not help but draw the comparison to the role Alec Baldwin played in the movie *Glengarry Glen Ross*, when he was screaming at the sales staff, that they should "always be closing!" All I heard was "always be clearing." Jon pointed to some dishes in the corner, he said, "Do you see those dishes, if you don't clear them no one will. Now start gathering plates!" When I sheepishly mentioned that it looked like people had just begun to eat, he told me "it did not matter, start clearing." I did. For fear of being fired I started clearing plates immediately. I was met with hostility instantly. "Don't take that" one lady snapped, when I tried to take her plate from under her. One indignant old man, when I reached for his plate, actually stabbed me with his fork.

My final post was the clearing shack. It was literally just that, a shack, set on the periphery of the party, where other tired caterers bussed a steady parade of dirty plates. My job was to simply separate, clear, and stack the dishes. I quickly got a system down. And was enjoying the work. This particular party had opted for the Texas barbecue menu, including succulent ribs. These things were magnificent looking. Some had barely been touched. Now what I'm about to say could be construed by some as gross, especially for a Hungerford-Nichols, but keep in mind I had no breaks, and aside for a couple of deviled eggs that I managed to jam down my throat when no one was looking, I had not eaten. I waited for just the right rib to pass by (the one I chose could not have had more than one or two bites out of it at the most), stuck out my head to make sure the coast was clear, and then made sweet love to that rib, yes I did. I sat down on a crate and gobbled it up with the passion of Lindsay Lohan's lesbian lover. It tasted so good, that if what I was doing was wrong, I did not want to be right. All was right with the world, I was at a Hamptons party, and I was getting mine.

SECOND TRIP TO THE DOCTOR

Once again, I found myself on the doctor's couch. Once again the doctor told me my problems were physiological and my frontal lobe was in desperate need of stimulus. This time I agreed to an amphetamine-Klonopin mixture.

From the doctor's office I went directly to the pharmacy. Twenty minutes later I was in possession of a large bottle of Ritalin. I had told the doctor that I was an alcoholic and drug addict, and he assured me that the amount I would take (five milligrams every four hours) was not addictive. However, when I got home and looked at the tiny little five-milligram tablet resting on my fingertip, I instantly convinced myself that five milligrams simply was not going to cut it. After all, I knew my system.

I had heard that the average adult was on a twenty-milligram cycle, so I would take half of that. I was on the subway when the buzz first hit. It was an absolutely blissful feeling of liberating clarity. I straightened my posture and pulled out a book from my cluttered book bag and began to read like everyone else around me. When I got to the computer lab at Columbia University, where I often went to write, I paused before entering.

I had a candy bar in my hand. Rather than walk into the lab with the chocolate in direct violation of the no-food rule, as I always used to do, I found myself *finishing* it *before* entering. Even more, I threw the wrapper *in the garbage can* instead of jamming it into my pocket. When I entered the computer lab, no one scolded me for eating as someone always used to do. Without a doubt the Ritalin was making me more civilized.

Before I began to write, I noticed my filthy knapsack. This annoyed me. This simply would not do. I took the bag to the bathroom and emptied the contents, which included everything from outdated newspapers to rotten banana peels. I *threw out* the garbage and *organized* the rest.

Writing, I *focused* on one paragraph until it was finished rather than jumping around from idea to idea. I was so impressed by the drug that I called my parents to tell them about my breakthrough. I had found a cure to all my problems.

I *worked* very deliberately and methodically, but then something dreadful began to occur. The buzz started to wear off. I wondered how this could be, for I had taken my magic pill only an hour and a half before. I looked at the clock and instantly became depressed to see that I had to wait two hours until I could take my next tablet of Ritalin.

I decided I could not wait. In the name of commerce and productivity I took another ten milligrams. Moments later I felt reinvigorated, but, sure enough, a half hour later I needed more. In three days I blasted though almost a month's supply of Ritalin. When I looked in a mirror I already saw a drug addict. I was gaunt and ashy.

Disgusted with myself, I grabbed the bottle, walked to a window on the eighth floor, and dropped it out the window. My self-esteem improved instantly. I was now back to recovery. The next day I awoke and felt depleted again. I went to Columbia to write and found myself in a listless state and could not write. I began to think of the Ritalin that I had thrown out the night before. Perhaps one pill could help me get going? The addict in me had awakened.

I ran down eight flights of stairs to get the dope. Construction workers filled the area below the window from which I threw the bottle. I did not bother giving them an excuse as I fell on my hands and knees in search of a pill among construction debris. I was not able to find a single pill.

I wanted and needed more drugs, and that meant I had to go back to the doctor. This is no easy feat because doctors are trained to spot abuse. If you want to buy crack from a dealer, you can have a knife sticking out of your chest and so long as you have the money, you will get the dope. With a shrink you have to be much more stealthy. You cannot do or say anything that will betray the fact that you are indeed a filthy drug addict. You must cloak the fact in appropriate terminology and jargon: "Well, I was chatting with my internist and, since I am so productive and so civilized to the point that I have even begun to recycle, we—I mean he—feels I would do even better on a larger dosage."

Ritalin makes you lose weight. A lot of weight. I went home for Thanksgiving after a three-week Ritalin binge. I guess I looked gaunt, for everyone kept staring at me with concerned looks throughout the meal. Finally, my stepbrother carefully broached the subject and asked if I had lost weight. "Yes, actually about a hundred pounds. Please pass the potatoes," was my only reply.

Ritalin is speed. The differences between speed and crystal meth are negligible. Ritalin abuse is far more insidious than with a street drug like crystal meth. Anyone who uses crystal meth is an overt druggie. Anyone who picks up Ritalin is just a functional person. Ritalin is insidious and evil precisely because it offers legitimate benefits. In World War II, fighter pilots were given Ritalin or speed to enhance their performance. How does one argue with a drug like that?

In some ways, I have tremendous respect for Ritalin. It can turn an unemployable person into a jobholder, an outlaw into a citizen, or a slob into a fop (good SAT word). Unfortunately, for me the stuff is simply too easy to abuse. A friend of mine told me that he broke his leg skiing, and because he could not move around much, he was able to accomplish more. Since I already have a precarious and temperamental nervous system coupled with an addictive personality, I would probably be better off breaking my leg than going back on Ritalin.

Although I have not been on any prescription medication for several years now, Ritalin still beckons me to this day. I stay away from it one day at a time. I leave myself no time to take drugs or drink booze. I do this by staying busy and working hard.

I used to share my Ritalin experiences in AA meetings. Often, people came up to me to tell me that they remembered when I was on it and that I had been a real mess. This has always bothered me because I was never around people when I was on the drug. Ritalin provides almost instant clarity; one becomes very aware of wasted time. I always wanted to tell these people who claimed to have seen me on Ritalin that, when on Ritalin, I would have preferred interpreting Schopenhauer or conjugating French verbs to chewing the fat with some drunk at an AA meeting. Of course, I would have tagged it with the ol' "No offense!" line.

I did stay on Klonopin (baby Valium) for three years. I am told a lot of people abuse this drug. I never did. The doctor gave it to me it for general anxiety, but he never asked me about my caffeine intake, and I never told him either. Here is some advice: if you are thinking about going on an antianxiety medication and you drink more than three cups of coffee a day, then you better modify your caffeine intake.

The problem with Klonopin and similar drugs is that they are powerful sedatives. Your body gets used to having it around and gets very *very* angry if you cut off the supply.

While on Klonopin I had planned a fishing trip to Costa Rica. (It ended up as a bunch of forty-year-old married guys fucking young native prostitutes. I did not participate. I hated the guys for it. I believe third world countries would, as a rule, like Americans better if we stopped fucking their children while on vacation.) Once in Costa Rica, I realized I had forgotten my Klonopin. At first I thought I could do without it.

The first few days off Klonopin are fine. There is still a reserve of it the body's system. The third day your neurotransmitters start to wonder where the fix is, but they give you a break, figuring that you are on the way to the pharmacy. However, by the fifth day, your brain cells are shrieking like deserted chicks in a nest or a guy thrown off a mountaintop.

After returning from Costa Rica, my first step was to the office of my neurologist to pick up new prescriptions for Klonopin and Ritalin. By this point, I had cut the doctor out completely and was giving a hundred bucks to her receptionist, who asked no questions, for the prescriptions.

I popped some Ritalin back at my apartment and picked up a *New York Times*. That is what I would do on Ritalin: read. Reading was so much more interesting on Ritalin. I inhaled newspapers and books as my scalp tingled with euphoria and hope. About every hour I dispensed another ten-milligram tablet of bliss. The prescription said every four hours. While I abused the Ritalin I did not abuse the Klonopin at all. I just wanted the detox to stop from the Costa Rica trip. I would take Klonopin when I was finished reading and wanted to go to sleep.

In total, I "slipped" or abused Ritalin three times. Two times, the slip lasted about ten days. The most recent time lasted only three days before I flushed the remaining pills down the toilet. I returned triumphantly to AA to count days again. Whether I had really slipped was a fun subject for my AA friends and me. Some said no, and some said yes.

"Only you can decide if you had a catastrophic slip or not," one friend told me. I remain uncertain. One thing for sure is that when I was on Ritalin, the pounds came off, mostly because I have to go to the bathroom every ten minutes or so.

BACK TO WORK: COMMERCIAL FISHING

People told me that I should be a comedian because I am funny. Then people told me that I should be a teacher because I am good with kids. I failed at both these occupations. So when those people told me that I should be a commercial fisherman because I love fishing, naturally I agreed. By the way, whoever wrote that book *Do What You Love and the Money Will Follow* should be beaten with a stick. I wonder how many ridiculous businesses were spawned by this absurd book.

The fishing community down at Shinnecock Inlet, New York, is composed primarily of third-generation Norwegian fisherman. I knew it would be a tough fraternity to break into. I had also heard that the squid fishing season was just about over and there was not a lot work to be had at the present time. Still, I loved the ocean and I was flat broke.

I was terrified of approaching the guys at the fishing docks. One glance was enough to show that these were real men who made a living with their hands. They were a little weathered from the elements, but they were well-built and strong. Not the bulky muscle of the guys at the gym. These men's muscles were less conspicuous and leaner. I had spent my summers at tennis camp, and though I was trying to conceal it, it was probably quite evident as well.

Much like the men, the boats themselves were built for industry. There was nothing recreational about these vessels. They were basically floating factories. Aesthetically, the boats were an atrocity. Real buckets of bolts, some of them had not seen a paintbrush in years. Everything was covered in rust. It did not look as though the boats were ever swept or washed. Nor did they need to be. Most boats at sea have a steady flow of water running through a hose. If that does not work, a rogue wave can give the boat a good rinse. Of course, fishing boats reek, but I like that.

However, all this dilapidation was sharply countered by the occasional presence of shiny new stuff. For instance, a huge rusty wheel had brand-new metal cable on it. A closer inspection revealed that the wheel bearings were new and freshly oiled. The radar and electronics were all a stark contrast to the weathered hulls. The nets and pulleys all seemed new and well maintained. In short, all the stuff needed to effectively slaughter massive amounts of fish was state of the art.

To my surprise, the men at the docks were not hostile toward me. In fact, some were rather cordial. I had been pumping a lot of iron then. I was also obviously equipped with a set of balls just to show up at the docks. I began to gain more confidence with every boat I solicited. I finally came upon a boat, *Allison IV*, where a bunch of guys were unloading boxes. A huge mass of an Italian guy named Peter asked me if I had any experience. I told him that I had had some limited experience working on charter boats, which was not a complete lie even though it was twenty years ago.

Then Peter asked me if I ever got seasick. (Apparently this was important.) I told him no. That was all he needed to hear. I learned later that a lot of very competent laborers come down for work, go out for one day, and return green and week-kneed as a newborn deer. Peter also asked if I would come out for one day without pay to see if I liked the work. I told him I would. He told me to report at three. I did not want to, but I had to ask whether he meant a.m. or p.m. He meant a.m. I biked home full of adrenaline. I was going to be a commercial fisherman!

When I arrived the next morning at three a.m., the place was silent. All I heard were some gulls and water lapping against the boat. I was not sure what do, so I just kind of paced around excitedly for a half hour. I jumped when the boat started up suddenly. It did not look like anyone was there. Apparently, Peter slept on board.

"Get on the boat," he said. Suffice it to say he was not as pleasant as he was the day before, not that he was boiling with kindness when I met him. He told me that he was waiting on another guy, but if he did not show in the next five minutes, he would leave him. The prospect of just me and Peter out on the high seas was terrifying. Just as Peter was ready to pull away from the dock, the other guy showed up. He was a young kid, maybe seventeen years old. We had a brief introduction: "This is Andy. Watch everything he does because you will be doing the same thing tomorrow by yourself," Peter bellowed.

To describe Andy as apathetic would certainly be an understatement. However, I suppose his indifference and aloofness were consistent with the profile of most seventeen-year-olds. He told me the job was no big deal and showed me how to pull the boat around using leverage and ropes. It was interesting as hell, how a propeller and a rope could work together to move such a huge craft. I was essentially getting a physics lesson. Commercial fishing, like most things in life, is all about leverage.

After we left the harbor, I expected that Andy would brief me on some stuff pertaining to what would go on once we got to the fishing grounds. Instead, Andy, obviously hung over, climbed into a bunk and went fast asleep for two hours.

I fell asleep as well, not in the bunks, which I would later fall in love with, but on a bench. It was wonderful to sleep. A combination of the rocking boat as it pushed through the waves and the steady drone of the engine was blissful.

I awoke as soon as I heard the engine shut off.

"Put your boots on!" Peter barked.

I did and went back to observe Andy. It was time to put the nets out. He was calm as only one who has done a thing a thousand times could be. Peter worked the hydraulic lift while Andy negotiated two enormous metal doors over the side of the boat. When lowered, the doors "dragged" along the ocean bottom, causing immense environmental destruction while they kept the mouths of the nets open to receive fish. The nets were let out via a couple of giant cables. That is how most people get killed on boats. A cable snaps and recoils, and if you happen to be in its way, it is curtains for you. Most fishermen are dead before they hit the water. Even if they were alive, their boots would instantly fill up with water, serving as anchors. The nets were put out around 5:00 a.m. while the sun rose indecently.

I was informed it would be a couple more hours before we would begin work. It was back to bed. This did not seem so tough a job after all. I settled into one of the bunks. Even with my horrible hygiene, the condition of the bunk was a little suspect. There was a distinct mildew/fish aroma. I could only imagine the amount of sexual self-abuse other fisherman had engaged in over the years in these quarters. However, once I settled in and heard that hum of the engine, what was once an unclean and purely utilitarian bunk was now a nurturing womb.

One hour later, the engine shut off again. I scurried on deck to observe Andy. This time we would bring the nets back in. Birds dove around the proximity of the nets as they came in. It was exciting indeed.

Peter pulled the net up by hydraulic lift and then dumped its contents into a big bin. What was in the nets? Squid. Thousand and thousands of squid (calamari). I was given gloves and instructed to separate the big squid from the little squid and to throw out any dead ones, "junk fish," crabs, et cetera.

This was it! This was that perfect job that I had been dreaming about. It was just like separating the balls and moving them from one bin to another. All I had to do was separate the big squid from the small squid. I jumped into that huge slimy bin of squid in a state of euphoria and began to diligently separate the squid, which were squirting black ink for some reason. I loved it. I was finally being industrious! I was a worker among workers!

After we separated the squid into different baskets (by the way, like the balls of my toy land fantasy, the baskets were red and blue), I dumped the baskets down a chute. At the other end of the chute, Andy iced and boxed the fish. It was industry at its best. A product that once swam was caught, boxed, and a day later, on sale at the fish market.

I noticed that Andy was starting to break a sweat down in the icy fish hole. When I mentioned it, he dismissed it as nothing and said I had not seen anything yet.

We were getting ready to put the nets out again, but the engine broke down. Both Andy and Peter went down to the engine room, leaving me in the kitchen area. I felt like such a pussy. The Men were trying to fix the engine with wrenches and other manly tools while I sat contemplating different curtain types for the kitchen.

Unable to completely fix the boat, we limped back to shore. On the way I heard Peter and Andy laughing up on the bridge. Peter was an incredible racist. Every other word out of his mouth was "nigger." I like to pride myself on not being racist, but I do know a couple of really effective racist jokes. Knowing how important it was that these guys liked me, I felt that if I went up there and told them a couple of good racist jokes I might become instantly ingratiated to the fishing community.

This could save a lot of time in the long run. I fancied it a sort of political move. So I climbed up to the bridge and let loose my best racist joke. It was received without so much as a smile. Apparently they were not ready to let me into the group. I did not mind and quietly retreated back down the ladder.

Once back, we unloaded our few boxes of squid and I went home. Peter told me to come back at three the next day. This time, I did not ask a.m. or p.m.

The next day there was no Andy. Instead, to my horror, it was just Peter and me. I jumped on the boat, trying to remember just some of the stuff that Andy had made look so simple. Everything started to collapse at once. Peter started the boat and told me to remove the stern rope. I looked to the back of the boat (I knew that much), where seemingly hundreds of neatly coiled ropes lay. Rather than ask which rope, I guessed.

"Not that rope, you idiot, the other one!" The theme of the day.

As a recreational fisherman, I had observed many trawlers in the past. And while I had always been told that fishing is the hardest profession in the world, I had never seen anyone working all that hard. What I did not realize was that there was always some poor bastard below deck in the "fishing hole" working his balls off.

Somehow Peter and I managed to get the nets out. I would get it right one time, but screw it up the next. I think that I could have gotten it down with time, but Peter had no time to let this dyslexic catch on. He screamed and screamed and screamed. Of course, the way things go, the more Peter bellowed, the more I messed up.

To add to my incompetence and nervousness, I also began

to have ethical questions regarding the entire operation. I am not an environmentalist by any stretch. In fact, I don't even recycle. But, even I, a slob, raised my eyebrows at the waste. We were no longer fishing for squid. Rather we had changed nets and were now targeting a specific breed called "weakfish." The nets dragged up everything on the bottom. Only the weakfish were kept. Everything else was thrown back dead. Hundreds and hundreds of pounds of beautiful striped bass, fluke, porgies, sea bass, sharks, probably a dozen species in all, were killed by suffocation on the deck.

We were now only a half mile off the coast of Fire Island. Because of the aquatic extermination I was witnessing, I was acting weird and Peter was on to me. I knew I had to focus; I had to stay on task. All I wanted to do was emancipate the dying fish. But I could not. Peter had already seen me throw back a couple of big bass and was furious at that. I felt like a soldier ensnared in a hideous war crime of genocide. I knew I had to keep killing in order to save my own skin.

There was one humorous part to all this when we went out for a three-day trip. Early on, Peter pointed to a red bucket with a rope on it and told me that if I had to take a shit to use the red bucket. I laughed, figuring he was joking. Since we had only been taking day trips, I had not found it necessary to relieve myself.

One morning, I turned the corner, expecting to see my usual beautiful sunrise. Instead, all I saw was Peter perched squarely on that little red bucket. His three-hundred-plus pounds tested the structural integrity of that bucket. My trippy mind began to think of the fate of that poor bucket. When it came off the assembly line, what were the statistical chances that it would end up getting violated on a daily basis by a tremendous Italian man? Could there be a worse fate for a bucket? When this red bucket was on the conveyer belt, all sparkly and new, the bucket before it would probably only have to endure at most a little too much bleach. The one behind it would maybe have to carry around some abrasive gravel on occasion. But this particular bucket would endure a massive man's shit.

At one point I thought, in fact I knew, that Peter wanted to kill me. And he had so many opportunities to do so. He could have easily pushed me overboard and reported it as one of those "accidental" deaths that happened now and then.

"It's too bad. He was a good kid," Peter would say to my grief-stricken parents.

I decided that it would be better, given the opportunity, to strike first and kill Peter. At one point when I saw his enormous body bent over the side of the boat trying to mend a net, the crack of his ass exposed, I realized that I should push the fat fuck overboard. Luckily, as quickly as that thought came to my mind, another thought came: What if I missed? I had a vision of the movie *Deliverance* and opted to abort my mutinous plan.

I was not fired from this job. I probably would have been, but the fact that I did not get seasick carried a lot of weight. I told Peter I was going to take a couple of days off. He called after a while, and I told him that the job was not for me. I never even asked about getting paid. Instead, I typed up an article about my experiences and sent it to a national fishing magazine. It was published in the next issue. I certainly can't show my face around Shinnecock Inlet anymore.

THE Fisherman

October 19, 2000 - No. 42   Long Island, Metropolitan, NY Edition $1.50

WIN A HYDRA-SPORT 2300 DREAMBOAT FISHING CONTEST

editor's **LOG**

COMMERCIAL FISHING BY-CATCH...LEGAL OR WASTEFUL?

We have heard for years about by-catch waste aboard commercial draggers targeting a specific specie. Here's another letter to further confirm the total devastation these vessels have on our marine resources under current practices.

Although these commercial anglers were within legal limits of the law, is what they are doing prudent? And, why can't our regulating officials come up with a solution to stop the mass destruction these vessels are capable of?

Dear Tom,

I spent the last month working on a commercial dragger a one-half mile off the coast of Fire Island. While I loved the work, and respect the skill and industriousness of the fisherman, as a recreational fisherman, I was alarmed, and shocked, as any sport fisherman would be, by the number of fish that were wasted and thrown overboard dead. Including thousands of pounds of striped bass and fluke, along with many blackfish and sea bass.

In short, the problem is that no real law is being broken. The "fishermen" are not keeping illegal fish, they are throwing back, as the law says, short fish, and endangered fish. The problem is that they are throwing the fish back dead.

I could see having a few hundred fish killed in the name of capitalism, but I am not talking about a few hundred, I witness nothing short of carnage, thousands and thousands of pounds of beautiful sport fish thrown over dead.

As the reader may already know draggers do not discriminate, they drag along bottom and pull everything in its path. A typical tow will yield 20 different species of fish. IE (shad, Spanish mackerel, bunker, weakfish, sharks, dog fish, porgies, kingfish, stripers, blues etc.). Many fish are kept and sold, this I have no problem with. However, it is naive of the government to think that the fish that are considered endangered or "off limits" are thrown back dead! Here is a news flash..."they are thrown back dead!"

My fear is if the government does not modify these ridicules, ineffective, limits, perhaps Long Island will become barren of fish like the waters off Japan are today.

I should also note, that I am far from an environmentalist, actually, I do not even recycle. I have caught bass using illegal short flounder. I say this to make the point, that the waste would have to be pretty substantial to raise the eyebrows of this particular slob.

While I am being honest I might add, being that I have never caught a weakfish I could not care if the entire population of weakfish were wiped out. However, I have spent too many hours trying to catch bass and fluke to see them pointlessly killed by the thousands is tough to take.

What happens, for those who do not know, is that the nets are brought in after hours of raking the ocean floor. The fish hit the deck alive, but in the name of commerce and productivity, all the energy is directed towards putting the nets back out to catch more fish. As the nets are being put out, the non-targeted fish are forced to suck on air for 20 minutes. As I see it, if the "fisherman" took three minutes to throw back some of the live fish it could make a big difference. Aren't these guys ultimately hurting their own resources?

My Question is who is to blame?

The commercial fisherman is not braking any rules. Does the government really believe that the 15-inch weakfish are being thrown back alive? Why have the laws at all? Would it be better if they were allowed a certain poundage regardless of size limit? I mean sure short fish would be killed but aren't they killed anyway?

In summary, I believe that the ocean should be harvested. There are, as any good recreational fisherman can tell you, plenty of fish out there (at least on the south shore). There is enough for both recreational and professional fisherman. I also know that most fishermen, including the guys I work for, while far from saints, are, talented and extremely hard working men, who risk there lives so that people like you and I can order fish off menus in NYC. However, speaking not as an environmentalist, but as a recreational fisherman, throwing back, hundreds of trophy fish, including many 40-pound cows, and 10-pound doormat fluke, seemed to be a waist. Am I wrong?

Some readers might feel that I am exaggerating; I really wish that I were.

Jeff Nichols

Managing Editor
Tom Melton

THE HOUSE

As I have established, fishing could get me into trouble. All my life I have fished through the ice for lake trout and whatever else was down there. Then there was the time I took my stepfather's car without asking (distorted sense of entitlement) and went up to his house overlooking a pond in upstate New York. I would love to tell you it was just a summer home or cabin, so I could dismiss the incident as just another funny story. However, the house had tremendous charm, and what followed is a sad and unmitigated tragedy that strained and damaged my family. The only good thing about what happened is that no one got killed.

I headed upstate to do some ice fishing on the pond in front of my stepfather's house. I should also mention that I was in a bad emotional state at the time. I had been experiencing some weird physical symptoms that had me very concerned (specifically, a burning sensation in my groin area). I was also projecting about a big upcoming comedy show and felt a need to isolate myself.

After I arrived at the pond, I was surprised to find there was no ice despite it being the middle of January. So, not wanting to drive back to Manhattan immediately, I went inside the house to take in a couple of football playoff games.

I did not want to turn on the furnace and cause a noticeable spike in the heating bill, so I retrieved the space heater and went into the basement where there were a couple of throw rugs, a couch, and a giant screen TV. The house was freezing so I put the space heater close to me; nothing knocks me out more than watching a game on TV on Sunday. I fell asleep before the first quarter was up.

I did not want to turn on the entire heating system, not because it would be an expensive waste of heat for one person, but because as I mentioned, the rise in the gas bill would tip off my parents to the fact that I had been in the house. My parents were in the midst of trying to wean the kids, specifically my sister and me, off the house, but if I had called my parents, who were vacationing in Florida, they probably would have given me the green light to use the house. I did not make that call, regrettably. When I awakened, the sun had broken through the clouds, and started to hit the sliding glass windows that served as an entrance to the basement. The "solar" effect had warmed up the house considerably. Feeling that the heater was too close, I turned it away from me, facing it toward the couch. Stupid move, I know, but I hate heat. Heat makes me claustrophobic and my body begins to twitch, which sets off my debilitating hypochondria and "Tourette's."

I nodded off again. The next time I woke up, I saw and smelled smoke. One of the couch cushions was smoldering. I felt I was in no danger. In fact, after I unplugged the offensive villain I sat and watched the cushion smolder for about five more minutes. (I know what you are thinking: space heaters don't burn buildings down, people do. Good point.) Finally, I retrieved a glass of water from the kitchen and threw it on the cushion. It made the typical hissing sound of flames being doused and the smoke dissipated. At this point, I should have dragged the whole couch outside and called the fire department, but I did not.

Instead, being the sneaky little bastard that I am, I then tried to see if I could cover up or hide the burn mark. I turned over the cushion, but that did not work. I really did not want to call my parents and tell them about the incident, but it looked as if

I might have to. My parents would be very disturbed about the cushion. I certainly did not want to use the words *fire*, or *smoke*, or any other alarming terminology that would add more fuel to the situation. I tried to come up with a benign description of what happened, so I settled on the word *singed*. "Hi, Mom, do you know that pillow on the basement couch? Well, I singed that, and also the five-mile-radius around the pillow is slightly singed too."

The only reason why I still sleep at night is due to the following: before I left the house three hours later, I noticed that the cushion was still warm, so I went into the kitchen and filled up three huge pitchers of water, probably close to five gallons' worth, and poured all of it into the burn hole. (I do recall that the hole was substantial and very charred.) I soaked that motherfucking cushion real good. I mean, I drenched it. There was water all over the floor. When I left the house, the notion that the thing was not out did not cross my mind. (I know. I should have taken the couch outside or called the fire department.) The house did smell like smoke when I left but I did not see any smoke—my only concern was that it would not air out before my parents returned.

At ten p.m. that night, my stepbrother Mike was the first one to tell me that the house was on fire.

"How bad is it?" I asked.

"Put it this way, they are focusing on the trees around the perimeter of the house," was his sarcastic reply. Truthfully, Mike was great throughout the ordeal; he constantly provided much-needed comic relief, like the fool in a Shakespeare tragedy.

The next day my stepfather and mother came back from Florida. Together, we took a relatively long two-hour drive up to the house from Manhattan. I spent most of the time on a car phone repeating to various lawyers and insurance agents exactly what had happened. I was very candid and told the truth. When asked why I did not call my parents to ask permission to use the house, I admitted that I did not want them to know I was there.

The site was awful; the house was completely destroyed. Even the cast-iron log holders in the fireplace were melted into little unrecognizable balls. Though I came close to sobbing I did not. I became detached from the situation, an observer instead of a participant. I remember watching my mother with ash on her face trying to salvage anything—half of a photo album, a few dishes, anything that was not scorched. I remember neighbors coming over and their behavior. Some looked scared while others, such as the actor-writer Spalding Gray, looked pensive and alarmed. They consoled my mother. I saw the whole mess as if I were floating above it and looking down at myself, some dumb-shit kid who burned his family house down. The cleanup began. For this we used a little black pickup truck. Luckily, there was an old barn on the property in which we could store the salvageable stuff. We made countless trips with a bunch of charred shit to be stored and later sorted through. It was a grueling process. A couple of times it was just my stepfather and me in the truck.

> Dear mom.
> How are you. I'm fine and getting ready for cornell. have you found out about. it yet should I speand the night at home with Jen. I dont no plase write back or call.
> love geff.

"So what did you guys talk about on the ride?" Mike, as always the wiseass, would ask. When I could not find the keys to the truck, Mike would taunt me, "If you don't find those keys, my dad will be very mad at you!" I had just burned down the poor guy's house! What were lost keys compared to that? He maxed out on anger.

By the way, I hate all volunteer firemen. They all suck. Every day during the cleanup, volunteer firemen would show up at the site to show their girlfriends the inferno they had "battled." Apparently, after receiving a phone call from two passersby about smoke coming out of the house two firemen arrived at the scene. Though the early stages of a fire were under way, the building had not yet burst into flames. Instead of heading to the rear of the house as they should have, the firemen opened the front door, creating a "backdraft." Fire needs oxygen to thrive. A backdraft occurs when fresh air is mixed with an intense amount of heat. The result is an explosion. Basically, the house erupts into an inferno.

The two firemen tried to battle the intense flames, but they ran out of water. Ran out of what? The house was fifty feet from a huge pond. Upon this realization, the firemen turned the truck around and, on their way back down the road, ran right into another fire truck coming up the hill. No one was hurt, but during the time it took to move the trucks the house burned out of control.

Remarkably, there was one dish that was untouched by the fire. It was not my mom's fine china or silverware, all of which was destroyed. Rather it was a cheap imitation porcelain dish with a tag on its bottom that said "Made in Taiwan." This cheap plate has now become our family's only heirloom. After the fire I promised my family that I would receive help. My experience with this, I believe, depicts the vast differences in therapeutic approaches, and how ultimately random it is to find a good shrink. I had no money, so I went to a clinic in the East Village. As in an HMO, I always find doctors at clinics to be patronizing.

"Why are you here?" my appointed therapist asked.

"I accidentally burned down my parents' house," I replied.

"Oh my God! That is the worst thing that I have ever heard of. You must really hate your parents on some deep level!" she shrieked.

Ultimately, my grandfather agreed to pay for treatment. This time I found a private psychologist who was the polar opposite of the first "doctor" I visited.

"Why are you here?" he asked.

"I accidentally burned down my parents' house," I replied.

"Shit happens," he said coolly.

I suppose the true answer lies between the two.

I would share about the fire at AA meetings, but I would always leave out the word *accident*. I think people believed that I doused the place with gasoline and lit a match. No one ever came up to me after those meetings.

Thereafter, I found it difficult to find people to identify with. Once in a while, some idiot would tell me that he and a friend had burned down his parents' garage with sparklers in the third grade. These confessions provided no real comfort. I needed to find someone who had done the exact same thing.

Finally, a comic friend of mine told me about a very eccentric female alternative performer who happened to be a heroin addict with a similar experience. I tracked her down after a performance and told her I had heard through the grapevine that she had once burned down her parents' house and that I had just

Before

Three days after the fire.
It looked like the Hungerford Castle in England.

done the same thing. To my amazement she said nothing. She simply stared at me till I walked away. I later discovered she had burned down her parents' house on purpose.

The fire was a devastating blow to my self-esteem. For years, all I said was "Excuse me" to people without any reason. "Excuse me" or "I'm sorry" rolled off my tongue at least ten times a day. I was in a hyper state of trying to excuse my existence.

Why is it that people have contempt for "do-gooders" or people who apologize too much? I felt like Felix from *The Odd Couple* when he tries to help an old lady cross the street and she hits him with her purse. I had become a groveling people pleaser, utterly incapable of setting boundaries or sticking up for myself. I avoided confrontation at all cost and even had a tough time making eye contact.

I tried to laugh off the fire for years. After 9/11, when New York City stunk of smoke, I could not help but think of that beautiful house and the destruction I had caused. Everyone in NYC experienced loss, but it was a personal battle for me to keep my self-esteem up. I was not a terrorist or an agent of destruction. Or was I? I have since settled for the fact that I am simply a sloppy, preoccupied guy with a handful of impairments who happened to burn down a house. I remind myself that I am still capable of helping others.

BACK TO WORK: FINALLY, JOB SATISFACTION

I did not fold after the house incident, though I really felt like crawling under a rock. I pushed on. I taught (well, showed up) as a substitute teacher for five straight weeks. I was on time and volunteered to help after school. Subbing was not really a job, though, but trying to keep the kids on task and, more important, being in the room distracted me from my depression. I had just about given up on ever working again. Listening to friends who insisted that I "go on with my life," I tried to do comedy two weeks after the house burned down. It was an audition for the Conan O'Brien show and I completely bombed. Because it did not look like I was going to be in my grandfather's will (no Brinks truck, after all), I even entertained the idea of applying for disability. I was disabled, wasn't I?

That summer, a construction worker named Gerry offered me a job at a site up in Carmel, New York. I told Gerry that I had been fired from a lot of jobs. Most jobs actually. I remembered all of my horrific painting experiences with Nichols Enterprises. I also told him I would probably become a liability for him. This guy knew I was a good tennis player, an adequate basketball player (who hustled), and that I was capable of working hard. He assured me that he had the perfect job for me, and, as it turned out, he did.

We were to lay a foundation for a new house in a very rural area. The first day of work, Gerry pointed to a stack of piled wood and told me to begin to transport it to the site. It was simple, and I worked hard. I moved the entire pile in a day.

Gerry was happy, and my self-esteem grew. I worked with Gerry all summer. I laid cement, shingled a roof, and ran errands for him in his truck. I had finally found success! There is something so wonderfully nurturing and satisfying about manual labor. Unfortunately, I'm all thumbs with a hammer and have a bad back, or I would be working on a construction crew right now.

IN AWE OF THE MUNDANE

I should mention another accomplishment that completely built up my self-esteem: I got back my driver's license, which had been suspended because of unpaid tickets. It was not a deed that I thought would validate me, like making it in show business or getting a beautiful girlfriend. It was much less glamorous, yet it was still oddly satisfying. I got my driver's license back!

Still, getting it back and keeping it was no small accomplishment. Because of my unmitigated slothfulness, I had let my license expire, which meant that I had to be retested. From my days driving around with *Laugh, You Lose*, I also had a trail of tickets (twelve) from all over the country (including North Dakota, a state with no centralized motor vehicle department) that I had to clear up. I originally thought that cleaning up my driving record would be a mundane chore with an incomprehensible amount red tape, which it was, but it also turned out to be a spiritual pilgrimage back to civilization. In the process of dealing with endless phone calls, faxes, trips to the motor vehicle department, and, worst of all, waiting, I became a better person.

Anyway, after a couple months of paperwork, I was finally able to register again for the written test. As I have established, like all learning-disabled people, I am horrible at taking standardized tests. The last standardized test I had taken was the scuba diving test, which I failed three times before the instructors allowed me to take the test orally. I did not think that the Department of Motor Vehicles would be as accommodating.

Waiting in line to see if I passed was nerve-wracking. I sweated like Mike Tyson at a spelling bee. Brooke, the pleasant sixteen-year-old ahead of me, received 100 percent on her test. I was genuinely happy for her. Yay, Brooke!! Then, it was my turn at the window. At the time, I could have missed six out of twenty questions and still have passed. I ended up missing only two. I was euphoric.

Throughout the twenty-mile bike ride back to my house I was downright giddy. (I had huge legs at the time, from biking everywhere, by the way.) I was on my way to becoming a part of the Establishment. A licensed driver.

Like a sixteen-year-old, I immediately called my mother.

"Guess what, Mommy?"

"You sold your screenplay!"

"No, I passed my permit test!"

"Oh, that's fantastic!" She was overjoyed.

I was thirty-seven.

I heard a long time ago in AA that "God is in the details." If one takes care of the little things in life, the big things will take care of themselves. I felt all was right with the world.

I wish I could say that shortly after getting my driver's license I woke up one morning suddenly organized and employable, but I cannot. It frustrates me that the drugs out there for people like me, drugs that can make me more organized, efficient, less slothful, and more civic minded, do not gel with me. I have to remember that I was in a bad place when I took Ritalin, a real addict.

I stand in wonder of highly functional people. Not millionaires or movie stars but people who just seem to be able to get the custodial aspects of their lives accomplished. Paperwork is still a drag for me, though I am much, much better. I do not owe the IRS a dime, and I am in full compliance. It is not that

I am lazy or merely hate doing paperwork. I believe paperwork requires small-motor skills that I just do not have. I will spend eight hours helping a friend move, deliver bundles of the *Improper Hamptonian* newspaper three days in a row, or help a friend put a floor in a house, but, for me, going to the post office or mailing a money order is completely overwhelming.

Once I had to send three separate money orders out to different agencies: one to the IRS and two for old speeding tickets. On each money order I had to write down the violation number. Halfway into the task, I began to shake and sweat. There were too many variables: numbers, stamps, envelopes, receipts, et cetera. I barely finished. I cannot believe how hard life is from an administrative point of view. And the more stuff a person has, the more paperwork comes at that person. My difficulty with these everyday activities makes me stand in awe of functional people.

I still sneak into gyms (but, as I've said, not the YMCA). I have been arrested twice for jumping over subway turnstiles. Both times I had to spend the night in jail because I had other outstanding tickets. I actually liked jail, not only for the obvious anthropological reasons, but also for its structured routine. Regardless, getting out of jail was so liberating that I skipped down the street. The last time I skipped down the street was in high school after I had just gotten blown by Lisa Silverstone.

To compound my troubles, my neurological problems are starting to bear down on me like a freight train. I just hope they stay at bay for a little while more. One day, I was so angry at missing a train and having to wait thirty minutes on the platform that I almost blurted out the two most offensive words in the English language, the words that every human being has lodged in a dormant database (or maybe not so dormant) somewhere. Even Mother Teresa, if pushed to her limit (e.g., stuck in traffic or a long line at Bloomingdale's) would have used these words. Granted, since Mother Teresa had years of spiritual development, it might have taken her longer to summon the offensive words than it would me.

A friend of mine who works on a mental ward of a hospital (the flight deck) confirmed my theory that when people lose their minds, the most common words they use are *nigger* and *cunt*, sometimes both at the same time in a sort of harmony "cunt nigger!" or "nigger cunt!" These words don't originate from a place of racism or sexism. They are simply the most shocking and offensive words anyone could ever use.

The funny thing is, as bad as the words are—and they are bad—when you are finally so pissed off at the world and the way it has treated you, so cross at the lack of quality pussy, that you let loose the last words in your arsenal, people just laugh at you. It's bizarre, but people tend to laugh at the person screaming *"cunt nigger,"* which only makes the screamer more enraged by his own impotency. Clearly, a man has no power if he yells the two most offensive words in the English language and everyone just laughs. A man has no power and he is clearly bonkers.

The train finally came and I had not blurted the gruesome twosome. *Thank God.* Although I did walk to the very end of the platform and yell "Comeon! Comeon! Comeon!"

As for the New Balance sneaker thing, the shoes do not seem to paralyze me as much these days, mainly because they are everywhere. I have been forced to exist with them. AA and its relentless effort to instill ego deflation has helped me enormously with this. I once heard a woman at a meeting say she modified the serenity prayer from "accept the things I cannot change" to "prefer the things I cannot change." This small modification has made a big difference in my life and has probably kept me out of an institution.

One of the primary "suggestions" of AA is that alcoholics avoid the "people, places, and things" that could trigger a relapse. Sage advice surely. I have always had a bit of an irreverent attitude about this advice. Yes, a crackhead should stay away from a crack house, certainly. To demand that an alcoholic stay away from alcohol is a tall order. Alcohol, as awful and destructive as it can be, is woven into the fabric of our culture. To constantly run from it is a preposterous notion.

What's more, though I have attended AA meetings for sixteen straight years, I am not really sure whether I am an alcoholic. For what it is worth, I never really completely embraced the whole disease concept that once an alcoholic picks up a drink, he will have an uncontrollable craving for more booze. Certainly, when I used to drink I would want more. But so does everyone else. Most people like to catch a buzz. I do not think there is a specific gene that alcoholics have. The only fact I know is that losers tend to drink too much. People who cannot figure out or do not want to figure out how the world works, people who do not really understand how hard and complicated life really is, often tend to drink too much. Or maybe it is the opposite. The people who know exactly how hard life is, how random it is, maybe they are the ones who drink too much. AA or no AA, people who drink too much should simply "put the plug in the jug."

I certainly drank like an alcoholic. I prefer to consider myself a nondrinker than a recovering alcoholic. It is much simpler saying you are a nondrinker. The thing about calling oneself an alcoholic is that it gives the word *alcohol* power over you. The word *alcoholic* implies that alcohol is still an issue. With an alcoholic there is always a threat that looms overhead: "Will he drink again?" An affirmative reply leads to: "Why did he start drinking again? Oh. That's right. He's an alcoholic and that's what alcoholics do. They drink."

Now, I, on the other hand, call myself a "nondrinker." That is, simply, I don't drink alcohol. There are millions of us out there. By definition, we do not drink by choice. A nondrinker cannot drink because—well, he is a nondrinker.

As a rule, most drinkers despise nondrinkers. In fact, a drinker would rather hang out with a reformed alcoholic than with a nondrinker because at least the alcoholic has had fun at one point in his life. But the teetotaler—no one likes a teetotaler. The drinker's attitude is: "Loosen up and have a drink."

As for me, I love a good drunk (drunken person, that is). I am attracted to good drunks like flies to shit. At the marina where I worked, there was a guy who painted boat bottoms and was a drunk by any definition. This poor bastard lived on an old houseboat at the marina, and he would get drunk, moon customers, and yell obscenities at his coworkers. The only reason he was not fired for his behavior was it is very difficult to find people to paint the bottoms of boats (very toxic). Instead, his coworkers would tie him up while he slept and dye his hair pink. It was so fucking funny but so fucking pathetic at the same time. Sometimes they would draw on his face with Magic Markers and he would not notice it until someone told him to look in a mirror.

I have not had a drink since 1990—I have also had very few sober days. I put down the drink and instantly picked up sugar, coffee, and cigarettes—all okay and sanctioned within the confines of sobriety. I get pie-eyed on coffee. It's not a drug, you say? My ass. Caffeine by any definition, by any standard, is a narcotic. Caffeine hits your central nervous system hard. I have done a lot of research on the subject (so could you just google it?), but to put it in layman's terms: Anything that makes you sweat, shake, and shit in your pants is a drug.

If a doctor told me to quit eating strawberries, I would have no problem with it. If the same doctor told me to quit coffee, I'd say, "Excuse me, bitch! Come again?!"

I was recently on the subway, and I was in a horrible mood. I was depressed about everything in life. I took the lid off my iced coffee and slurped it down. Euphoria hit, and I was one with the world. Complete bliss—hallelujah! Not mind altering? I am high and productive once the caffeine enters my system.

How else am I not sober? I am a self-seeking adrenaline junkie. I try to reach people through my comedy act. I get high on the laughs. My comedy is not about helping other people. I am like every other dude: I want to fuck hot chicks. (Luckily, the universe is on to my little game and has shot me down completely in that area.)

As bad as cancers and plagues are, for a man, there is nothing worse than the combination of age and career failure. I am looking at both these monsters right in the eye. Meanwhile, I am full of lust. Again, if there were a pill to wipe out what is left of my weak, drug-ridden libido, I would gladly take it. Or elective castration. Like a dog, I would look confused and be melancholy for a bit, but those feelings would wear off eventually. With lust out of the way, I may have years of untempered productivity.

To compound my anxiety/depression, Manhattan has the most beautiful women in the world (millions), and every time spring is in the air, these women wear revealing little sundresses. God help the man who pushes forty and is broke. He doesn't have a shot at any of them. I don't make the rules, but I sure as hell know them.

I also became a fishing junkie, which sounds funny but is really no joke. People have ruined their lives, marriages, jobs, and families trying to catch the elusive fifty-pound striped bass.

There are relatively few of us in this sport of hunting giant striped bass (say 2,000) on the East Coast. I am not including people who fish striper fish a lot. I am talking about the guy who wakes up at three in the morning in February thinking about what time the tide will change on the July full moon. I am talking about the postman who got fired for coming in too late and smelling of fish! Or me, who spent the majority of the money I got for the movie trying to catch big fish.

THE BEST TEST I EVER TOOK

I got the bug to be a charter boat captain early on in life. When I was about ten we'd spend time at my grandfather's enchanted summer home on Cape Cod (Harwich Port) and I would walk down to the docks and talk to the captains. A few times they would let me come along if it was all right with the charter. It was a long ride out around Nantucket to the shoals, and often when we got there, there was a pea soup fog. But once the bluefish and stripers started to bite, the action was fast and furious. I was bit hard with the fishing bug!

But becoming a captain myself had a catch: the Merchant Marine captain's exam, a tricky proposition by anyone's standards. Harvard grads have flunked this one, take my word, mainly because they took it for granted and didn't prepare.

As I have established, standardized tests are like kryptonite to the learning disabled. When I missed eighteen out of twenty questions on a captain's practice exam, I had severe doubts whether I could fulfill this dream. Still, I convinced my dad to pony up the cash for a four-week cram course that boasted it would increase my chances of passing to 90 percent. My only advantage in taking the test was that I knew preparation was key. The captain's exam is beautiful in that it does not discriminate. Effort equals success. An MIT grad with a master's in aerodynamics ain't passing this one without the proper study. Conversely, an average Joe with a modest education can pass with a lot of hard work. (At least, this is what I hoped.)

The cram course itself was mundane and boring. It mainly consisted of massive amounts of data you needed to memorize to pass the multiple-choice test. One tends to forget half of the stuff a week after the exam. A lot of it is outdated and redundant. Some of the safety stuff was helpful, but again there was too much thrown at you to memorize. The class did not go into enough practical detail (like why tides changed every six hours) to really get one acquainted with the material. By the end of the course I still did not have a clue about how to tie a slipknot. We did learn a little about navigation, however, and, miraculously, I found myself actually concentrating on the material. What's more, though it involved some convoluted calculations, I seemed to be learning it.

The course was designed to make it easy to pass a difficult

test, and to do this they furnished similar practice tests on their Web site. So I would sneak into a computer lab at Columbia University and take practice test after practice test after practice test. No one could have possibly taken more practice tests than I did. I literally studied twelve to eighteen hours a day for three weeks. I took the tests so many times that soon I was scoring over 90 percent each time I took them, at least on three of the four sections. But that fourth section was a bitch, involving plotting, i.e., straight math. This was overwhelming at first, a lot of military time and algebraic equations. But then I focused on the principles I learned from my high school math tutor, Mrs. Pavlac. Also my stand-up comic friend Dan Naturman helped me with the military time.

I had failed at stand-up comedy, in the business world, as an athlete, so I needed this paper showing that I was a captain to justify my existence and validate me. Captain Jeff Nichols.

The day of the test I sat next to a pleasant Asian kid who had breezed through the course. He also tore through the exam. He was done in under two hours. As I sat next to him trembling, twitching, and making audible noises; smoke may as well have been pouring out of my ears as my two brain cells banged together to come up with answers. I could not help but make comparisons with our culture. I was an American rock head, and he was a well-oiled machine. Calm, smooth, and efficient. It took me the maximum time, four hours, to finish the test. Of course, I failed the plotting section (math), but I went in to retake this section. I took another four hours. The end result? I passed with flying colors! Apparently finishing at the top of the class in one section, "the rules of the road," I got only one question wrong out of thirty.

Now I was really Captain Nichols. Afterward, I even began my own boat chartering business, aptly named Second Choice Charters. If the leaders of the fleet were already booked, there was always me. I also served as acting captain for Jimmy George, owner of one of the most storied boats in Montauk, the *Nicole Marie*, and the man who landed the second-largest mako shark in history and the third-largest striped bass on record (sixty-nine pounds).

My first year as a charter captain I made three thousand dollars while racking up five thousand in fines for various violations, and that is only a slight exaggeration. My primary customers were Guatemalan landscapers. They were all friendly guys, but not one of them knew a word of English, save for the guy who would put the trips together and he only knew a little. The only word in Spanish I knew was *rápido* (fast), which I would yell over and over again—"Rápido! Rápido! Rápido! Rápido!!"—as they tangled all my lines. They would pay me twenty dollars a head. Once I had six guys on my tiny twenty-two-foot vessel. These guys were tenacious fisherman, especially since they spent their entire time at sea puking. Not just one of them but all of them. Puking the entire time. When I got back to the dock I cleaned puke for two hours, and there were still spots of it the next morning.

Often we fished at night. I love that. I like to leave Montauk Harbor around sunset. As you come out of the harbor and you look to the west, the spectacular sunset behind Gardiners Island rivals anything the West Coast has to offer. As dusk fades into night, the stars appear like white shiny jewels on a black velvet cloth. The sky at night over Block Island Sound is magnificent, and night is also the best time to fish.

On some occasions when I was all alone returning from a successful night of fishing, I'd be driving into a cool north wind in a good mood, perhaps after catching a big one . . . I would start to fiddle with myself. The first time I did this I could not believe how aroused I got. Forget Viagra, I could have beaten a seal to death with my normally flaccid cock. I am telling you, a monkey could have swung from the thing. I was amazed and so proud, I felt like pulling up to another boat and showing it to the people on it. "Hey, would you look at this?" And they'd say, "Wow that's a nice one." As though I were showing them a fifty-pound striped bass.

So, I am a pig, yes. I am also an opportunist and I am not ashamed to tell any sailor to try it. Only when the north winds blow.

I prefer to use live bait like porgies, but we primarily use eels, which striped bass devour. On a full moon in July or August it is not uncommon to land several forty-pound fish. My two biggest to date are a pair of forty-eight-pounders, with fifty the goal to beat. The high-water mark! All striped bass junkies are hoping to land a fifty-pound cow. That's what we want, that's what most of us are after.

But if one thinks he can pass a captain's test and just saunter into Montauk, well, he probably could, but being accepted by the charter fishing community will not be so easy. I was the laughingstock of my marina for years. I was simply terrible at docking, crashing into everything to the delight and horror of the onlookers. When people found out that I was a captain and was running a service called Second Choice Charters, it raised more howls.

Being a mate is tough work. I love to fish, but I don't love hours and hours of cleaning up puke, and getting hit in the head with 16-ounce sinkers by reckless drunk firemen and cops; I would rather dig ditches.

Last year, as a charter captain with my own vessel I netted fifteen grand, but I charged (and spent) more than twenty thousand dollars trying to catch huge striped bass. I chased big fish with the same unbridled enthusiasm I chased chicks and drugs back in college. Catching big fish compensated for all my deficiencies. Basically, all us diehard bass fisherman have tiny pricks. Most of the money went to pay for fuel for my huge gas-guzzling engine. It is all basically big-shotism. Outboard motors should be banned. I did my fair share of putting a God-sized hole in the ozone layer. I am sure some kid in the Bronx has asthma due to my gas-guzzling stinkpot of an engine and the polar bears! The sad, irredeemable part of it is that I knew what I was doing. But with knowledge and awareness there is the chance of change. I really don't think the jackass you see riding around on a Jet Ski could give a shit about the environment. For the life of me, I could never see myself being friends with anyone who owned a Jet Ski. Or, for that matter, plays paint-splat ball every weekend in an organized league when there is a war going; I mean, have some respect.

Like any addiction, my fishing habit sometimes got me in trouble.

BOOTLEGGERS BEWARE! CONFESSIONS
OF A STRIPED BASS POACHER

When the dark green uniform of Montauk's legendary NYS Department of Environmental Conservation (DEC) officer, "Jerry Manfrini" (as we'll call him), harshly contaminated my peripheral vision in the parking lot of the Gone Fishing Marina, I froze. Sure, like a baseball player who just hit a pop fly, I went through the motions of running out the bases, knowing it was most likely a futile action. I continued, as instructed by the commercial fisherman who hired me, to pull the cooler containing eight illegal (untagged) striped bass toward the van. But by the unmistakable gait of Officer Manfrini as he approached me, I knew the jig was up. I was going down, and I was going down hard—and in a very public (the marina was packed with people) and conspicuous way.

For years the DEC has been cracking down on the flourishing and mercurial Long Island black market striped bass industry, and now I was in its crosshairs—someone they could string up and make an example of and possibly, if they tormented him enough, someone with information regarding a much larger and robust black market operation.

It is said that Officer Manfrini has generated more revenue via tickets and summonses than any other DEC officer in New York State history. Though he hadn't had a big bust in some time, he was still notorious for being perceptive, cagey, and manipulative. He did his job well. Brain dead from too much sun, I knew I was no match for him. I admitted to everything. I sang like a canary.

Now, as I said earlier, upon graduating from college twenty

years ago, if I had been able to look into a crystal ball and see that at forty years old I would be illegally selling fish out of a busted-down car, I would have hurled myself off a tall building. But, luckily, becoming a forty-year-old ne'er-do-well is incremental; it does not just suddenly come upon you like a bad case of the gout. Over the course of time, one makes enough bad career decisions until one day selling porgies from a cooler on the streets of Jamaica, Queens, seems like a completely logical way to pull down a living. It becomes the next right thing.

In the case at hand, I was working on a fishing boat for a licensed commercial fisherman authorized to sell the highly regulated bass. (Note: striped bass are *not*, by any means, an endangered species. Far from it, the fishery has recognized a complete recovery from the days of indiscriminate netting. Until the 1980s there were tons of bass taken in the nets. Since the nets have been banned, striped bass are abundant and, many believe, need to be harvested.)

The captain, my employer, was not from the Montauk docks but hailed from another port down the coast where they might not have observed the rules as strictly as Montauk skippers typically do. For whatever reason, he had *not* instructed me to put on the metal strips, called "tags," which had to be placed on every fish for regulatory and documentation purposes. This made them illegal.

I was sent by the captain with some of the illegal fish into the parking lot when I was approached by Manfrini and his posse, which included three police cars with lights on. If that wasn't overkill, in case there was an attempted water escape, there were three harbor patrol boats surrounding the marina. (I did not see any air support.)

Now, in an effort to establish complete candor, I am in no way an innocent "sports fisherman" who got caught up in a bad operation. I knew what this captain was up to. The problem was that I was addicted to fishing on my own boat (catching big fish validating, I suspect, compensating for, something). To pay for my huge gas bill, I had been selling fish to restaurants on my own for three years.

Frankly, it was a blast. I was a modest thief. I would go out at night, catch two fish (if I brought a friend, four fish), and then next day sell them to restaurants at five dollars a pound. Most of them weighed close to thirty pounds. You do the math. If I may offer a modest defense, I was never gluttonous. I could have taken ten fish a night without getting caught.

If I had been caught with my own modest two-fish-a-night enterprise, it would not have been so bad, but now I was caught up in a much bigger operation that extended from Montauk to fish markets and restaurants across Suffolk and Nassau counties right down to the Fulton Fish Market, then in Manhattan.

In the Manfrini case, reduced to the crudest and sexiest terms, I was asked to go in front of a grand jury and testify against the mob.

I am sure most look at my little bootleg operation as pathetic and contemptible, but my conscience is clean. I am not a "sport" fisherman. I have *no* interest in torturing an uneatable blue marlin for two hours then letting him go off to die or mounting him on a wall in an office. I like to catch fish and eat them. Just like that. I like cleaning and filleting fish, putting them on ice. I like the whole process, the industry of it. For the most part, I do not understand the finer art of fly-fishing, nor do I understand catch and release.

Beyond catching and cleaning, I began selling fish. I make a modest living as a writer, and selling fish became great supplementary income. Here was my day: fished all night off Montauk Point, returned with the two fish, iced them up, then went to bed. Wake up. Drive a few miles and get two hundred dollars cash for *fishing!!!*

I used go to the back of Japanese restaurants and haggle over prices. If the price was higher in NYC (sometimes up to six dollars a pound), I would go all the way into the city. Once when my car was broken, I called a cab and, with the help of the driver, loaded the cooler of fish into the trunk, then went to the train station, where the driver looked on in astonishment as I labored to drag a 150-pound cooler full of fish up a 100-yard ramp and onto the train, barely boarding before the doors closed. It might have looked dumb, but I had a great adrenaline rush. I was getting mine. I was a player.

Officer Manfrini was legendary for being able to extract the truth from fishermen. I knew as soon as he stopped me that any kind of lie probably would get me in a worse mess. I was also kind of relieved in a way, emancipated from my brief stint in the huge illegal striped bass market.

Probably sensing an easy kill, Manfrini was friendly at first. "Hi, are you coming back from fishing?" he said. He then asked to look in the cooler. I had no objections. Then he asked if my name was Jeff and had I gotten off this particular captain's boat. At that point, like Martha Stewart becoming aware that her broker had turned on her, I knew that this was a sting. I had been ratted out.

I was pissed only because I was a ridiculously small-time bootlegger, which sounds harmless enough until you realize that

60 percent of the striped bass sold in NY restaurants come from the black market, which obviously hurts legitimate commercial fishermen who count on striped bass for their livelihood.

Manfrini then walked me down to my employer's boat, which was circled by two harbor patrol boats, lights ablaze. Being that there was no cocaine trafficking involved, this seemed like a little much. The captain did not go down as easily as I did; he was actually a legitimate commercial fisherman and had a license to harvest striped bass. At first, in a desperate attempt to free himself from Manfrini's grasp, the captain tried to place the blame on me, which didn't particularly bother me. I chalked it up as a nice try. Maybe we'd both wriggle out of this. In front of maybe forty onlookers he pointed to me and bellowed: "I told that idiot to put the tags on the fish." I went along with his futile effort and, on cue, sheepishly bowed my head, hoping to convey innocent wrongdoing. But Manfrini would have none of it. "Bullshit. You guys are selling to restaurants and now you are caught."

As we stood on the dock, our body language screaming guilty, heads lowered in remorse, and circled by a growing crowd of inquisitive onlookers, Manfrini and his boys searched the boat and then had us empty our pockets, looking for contraband. This was particularly humiliating for me, not because I was carrying anything illegal, but colossal slob that I am, my pockets always contain a mess of wrappers, outdated receipts, and unexplainable pieces of twine. I also had a half a Snickers bar with quarters imbedded in it.

"That's gross," one of the officers commented.

"I am sorry, I am a bit of a slob," I countered, trying to endear myself with the group of officers.

At this point I was having kind of an out-of-body experience, like the "Want to get away?" commercial.

However, when I looked at the actual summons I was instantly shocked into reality. I was being charged with the same violation as the captain, with a five-thousand-dollar fine and a possible year in prison. The charge was for eleven untagged striped bass, even though we had caught only five, which was one over the limit. Apparently I was also being charged for a box of fish from the day before.

I was a good fisherman who made some impulsive, stupid decisions, but not all bad. As a writer I have published articles about fisheries conservation and the destructive effect of drag netting on various species. In fact, I got introduced to the striped bass black market as a subject while researching an article regarding fluke regulations for Screamingreel.com. I was as outraged as anybody and remember thinking, *What scumbags.* But then I heard the words that corrupted me: six dollars a pound!

I did not go out intentionally to catch and sell striped bass, but one night I was behind on some bills and knew how to pick up a couple hundred bucks with a rod and reel. I justified my poaching various ways: a) by purchasing bait and gas, et cetera, I put the money back into the economy; b) the flounder population would be protected by thinning out the abundance of bass that feed on them; c) the real enemy is the commercial draggers, not the guy with a rod and reel.

One time I saw a few teenage kids having a great time catching nice-size bass on lures off Montauk Point. As they, obeying the law, diligently threw them back, I resisted the temptation to pull up alongside them and corrupt them by screaming: "What are you doing!! You could get six dollars a pound for those things!!"

About a week before my court date I got a call from Manfrini asking me to testify against the captain of the commercial boat. That very day the captain also got a call from Manfrini asking him to testify against his "buyer." Now I was aware that this is how Manfrini got his info. He wanted us to rat just like we were ratted on. I felt like I was in the Gotti family.

For weeks after, it seemed all of Montauk was talking about the case. Everyone was scared that I was going to rat him or her out. I got several very real threats from restaurant owners and commercial fishermen. One guy waved a tire iron in my face. Appropriately terrified, I promised I would rat on nobody. The day of the trial the captain was called in front of the judge first. There the judge read out all of his violations in front of a packed courthouse. (Most people were waiting to pay or dispute parking violations.) Manfrini got him not only for the fish but numerous other violations ranging from a lack of registration for the boat to an illegal toilet aboard and marijuana possession. Every time the clerk read out a charge, the courtroom would collectively groan, "OOO." Or "O, God." One woman snapped "That's outrageous!" as if the guy were clubbing seals to death on Main Street.

I avoided prison but paid a thousand-dollar fine and one thousand for a lawyer. I am now a golfer and spend most of my free time insider trading, a much more respectable field. Just kidding.

ALASKA

Fishing: "It's not all about the glory."

Bored one afternoon when I was up at the computer annex at Columbia University last winter, I typed "captain jobs" into Google, and up came a bunch of jobs primarily in Alaska. Apparently, it is tough to get eligible captains (with valid licenses) up that way for just a few months out of the year to run charter fishing boats. Think about it, the guy could not really be married or have a full-time job—or any criminal record (one DWI in the last twelve months and forget about it)—he must be ready to pull up all roots.

Due to traffic congestion and increased fishing regulation on Long Island, it would be difficult to make any money as a mate in Montauk on Long Island this season. I knew that last year the harbor was down 60 percent. The idea of going to Alaska, our "final frontier," was so thrilling and wonderful: I would go to bed and dream about it. (By the way, Alaska is frigging huge, immense; I flew over a quarter of it; hundreds and hundreds of miles of tundra that literally has not been touched by man . . . I don't know . . . I believe in global warming and our very real contribution to it, and that alternative energy/conservation is the answer, but observing this vastness—dare I say drill for *oil*?)

A captain I know, Jimmy George, once told me that fishing was "not all about the glory." At the time, I had a very loose conception of what he meant—sure, you must spend time organizing and preparing equipment before you can actually fish, but this truism did not fully sink in until I got to Alaska.

When Captain Mike, the owner of the Alaska charter business that I signed on with, told me to come up a couple of weeks early for "prep work," I figured that I would get there, stay in a nice clean bungalow with a private room (possibly housekeeping service) overlooking idyllic mountain ranges, go to a couple of meetings with other captains, fill out some paperwork, learn the local fishing and nautical regulations, chat with other captains, fix some reels and tie some rigs, and practice on the boat. Then I would be free to do as I please in "nature's playground."

I had some romanticized notion of me, doing as I pleased and on my own a lot, whiling away the time before the tourists showed up. My scenarios always involved fly-fishing by a roaring river. I envisioned myself in a comfy hotel room with a good view. After breakfast, I could go for a hike then spend the rest of the day reading. In my *extremely* misconceived view, I was to do minimal work before the customers showed up. I kind of expected a turnkey operation: mechanics would do all the technical stuff, all I had to do was get on the boat, load the passengers on, and head to the fishing grounds.

Suffice to say, I was way off. The very day I arrived at the airport, I worked four hours moving parts to an old diesel engine off a boat after flying eleven hours. The next day I was up at seven and started working at seven-thirty: painting boat bottoms (I sucked), sanding, bailing out bilges, untangling ropes, helping, as best I could, with mechanical and electrical problems.

As it turns out, I was sent to the boatyard to work for two weeks. This work was brutal—lots of scrubbing barnacles off boat bottoms and using toxic cleaning materials for often sixteen-hour days.

In a spasm of candor, I had told Mike up front that though

I had a big heart, I had minimal experience as a captain, I was a little weird at times, and also that I was not handy at all. In short, I was barely a man. I assured him that I could change oil and maybe the batteries, but that was about it. I suppose, desperate for someone with a captain's license he told me not to worry about it, I would learn on the job.

We worked sixteen and eighteen hours a day for two weeks straight. Captain Mike ran a big operation. He owned nine boats: two large party boats about 50 feet long, and a bunch of smaller power boats about 28 feet long (these were the ones I would be driving). All the boats had to have the oil changed, hulls sanded and painted, and general prep work for an upcoming Coast Guard inspection.

When I told Mike that I was not handy, I don't think he really knew what I was saying. I think it would have been better/clearer to say that I was retarded . . . slightly . . . really.

While I was certainly out of my element, I did shine at the boatyards a couple of times, I must say. Once, Mike was working to fix a light fixture that had baffled the entire crew. None of their formidable tools could get at a finicky wire. No one knew what tool to use; at least three of them were working on it. At this point I fiddled in my pockets (where my hands always seemed to be) and came upon a pair of needle-nose pliers I had bought on Canal Street in New York City for a dollar. I decided to throw caution to the wind: not knowing if it would work at all, I interrupted the boys and said "maybe give this a try" as I handed them my new tool. To everyone's amazement it worked perfectly—it was the precise tool for the job! All the crew guys, who, by this point, were completely disappointed in me, looked at me in disbelief. I gloated.

Another time, the captain popped his head out of the engine room (I was the only one around, staring off into space, lost in profound thought, probably thinking of something along the lines of "If I shit multicolored ice cream, what would it look like?") and asked me to pass him a crescent wrench. Afraid to tell him I did not know what a crescent wrench was, I looked about and saw about six wrenches sitting on a counter, then randomly grabbed one. To my amazement and delight he told me thanks. I had picked the crescent wrench! (I could have just as easily handed him a lock wreck, or channel lock wrench, or an adjustable, or a shoe, but I picked the crescent!!)

Mostly, I was all thumbs. They would hand me a ratchet set or a corking gun and tell me to do such-and-such, and I would start do it, then screw it up. One time I got some sort of permanent ceiling composite all over a new engine, all the tools, and me. It does *not* come off hence the word *permanent*.

On another occasion, after I had gotten corking material all over, Mike (who had great patience) gave me an "easy job"—all I had to do was spray-paint the name of the boat (*Sunday*) on to the back of ten new life preservers. "Here is a can of spray paint and a stencil; take these new life jackets and stencil the name of the boat on the back of the life preservers." He added that it would be "tough to screw up that job."

Well . . . for starters, I did not shake the spray-paint can enough. Then once I had liberally filled in the holes that spelled the name of the boat, I stepped back to give them time to dry but failed to find them shelter from the wind. With one gust, a couple of stencils blew off allowing the watery black paint to leak and smudge all over the bright new orange preservers. When I was through, I lifted the stencil letters causing the paint to smear everywhere. It was another "Do you want to get away?" moment. I just sat there.

Note, very important: In an attempt to ingratiate yourself with the work crew, especially if you are not fitting in to begin with, and they are mad at you for not "pulling your weight"—(I overheard this), do *not* attempt to use outrageous humor to achieve this goal. For instance, do not imply that you are attracted to men in any way as a form of "shock humor." (Does not go over well with other crew members.) During lunch break, after most of the guys, who had been disappointed/shocked by my poor work ability, were decidedly not speaking to me. To put things in perspective, most of the crew had worked on boats their whole lives and the others were tree loggers from Oregon: TREE LOGGERS FROM FUCKING OREGON. In other words, they were real men.

I was being ostracized, but, I knew that a big play could change the game for me. It worked once for me already. My first day with the other captains they were talking about moose and how prevalent they are out here blah, blah, blah. So, sensing the timing right, I threw caution to the wind and tried the old "Moose Cock Joke." You know the one, where an old lady on a guess-the-word game show is asked, "If you can eat it?"—moose cock! The joke is always hit or miss, very risky—but delivered correctly, it can have a huge payoff. The first time it worked perfectly—everyone howled and I was in with the captains! But now I was not with the captains, but with a tougher lot of young, scrappy yardworkers. So I decided upon an old bit from my now dormant comedy act. With the air chewing of sandwiches in the background, I tried to defuse the tension: "Hey guys, let me get this straight, if you're more than 100 miles offshore, whatever happens between two men who are in search of comfort, is not considered gay, right? Do I have that right or is it 150 miles? I mean to me *Brokeback Mountain* was not a gay movie; it was more about survival on the lonely prairie." This got crickets, no one laughed. The guy sitting next to me moved over about a foot.

Another time, a new young guy showed up to work on one of the boats. For whatever reason he took off his shirt to put on another one. He was very ripped up and chiseled. I could not resist pointing to the kid and saying to the huge 300-pound redneck from Texas next to me "Mmm delicious!" "What the fuck!" the Texan belched as he moved away from me. Later, I heard the guys in the kitchen talking about whether I was gay or not. It got so bad that I had to start saying stuff like, "You guys know I was just joking . . . I hate fags." And, "Gay is immoral," et cetera. I am surprised I did not say: "Hey, let's go fag-bashing." This probably only made my lot worse. The entire time in Alaska I felt like I was on a reality show and I was the one that was about to be voted off the island.

After the boatyard I was sent to another location to clear out an old warehouse with two twenty-one-year-old guys, who were originally tree men from Oregon. They knew all there was to know about loading trucks and moving stuff. They were especially proficient at what and how to latch something down to the top of a car or inside of a truck. I am not being patronizing here: I was truly in awe of these guys' abilities. They used their minds very well. Very deliberate, very thoughtful. There was always a method to their madness: rather than simply lugging stuff around, they were always thinking two or three steps ahead. It turned out that both their fathers where in the construction business, and from an early age they had learned how to work with their hands. While they had a wild side, they were good kids. They were the type of kids that would make any parent proud. They were hardworking—one had been in the army and learned how to work on B-52 bombers. This, I must say, altered my opinion of an opportunistic army that exploited young recruits. You can leave the army with great skills, that is a fact. You can also leave dead or with one leg, that is a fact, too. But what they say in the commercials is not all BS. They will teach you skills you will not learn in college. I learned how to make a bong out of an apple in college. Complete waste of time. They learned directly marketable skills.

So to put a bow on this final little piece, let me list the reasons why I was fired from my Alaskan dream job: 1) obviously poor mechanical skills; 2) the owner flat-out did not like me; 3) I ran over a stop sign with a trailer while backing up a boat; 4) I was caught smoking cigarettes on the boat with customers—a no-no; 5) what probably put the final nail through the coffin—when it was my turn to pick out videos from the store, I chose *Grizzly-man*. Now, I thought all the hunters in the lodge would like a good old-fashioned bear story. I thought it was about some guy fighting off a vicious bear, but as it turns out, the film was made by a bleeding-heart, anti-hunter animal lover. Halfway through the film Mike asked who got the video, and I had to raise my hand. He shook his head and the next day I was headed back to New York City.

HOW A SLEAZY, "LEARNING-DISABLED" ROAD COMIC/FISHERMAN GOT A MOVIE MADE ABOUT HIS LIFE

So maybe you're wondering about this movie I talked about at the beginning. That's right! A movie, *Trainwreck: My Life as an Idoit*, based on this book, has been made and hopefully will be released soon. It was in the Seattle Film Festival and won an award at Michael Moore's Traverse City Film Festival and was well received by audiences at both places. *Variety* magazine gave it a great review.

Trainwreck stars Seann William Scott, Gretchen Mol, and Jeff Garlin and depicts how as a privileged child on the Upper East Side of Manhattan, I was confined to special education, ultimately became a substitute teacher in the South Bronx, and had a lot of other jobs along the way.

As I said at the outset, a major indie production company, This Is That, optioned the rights to my unpublished book. Having won at Sundance a couple times and produced many acclaimed independent films, This Is That is in a position to be selective. They do only two or three movies per year. The last book they helped adapt was by John Irving.

Personally, I wouldn't have made the same kind of film that emerged from my own book, but I am fully appreciative of my incredible good fortune. A major indie picking up the unpublished work of an unknown author? Truly miraculous!

So, how did the movie thing happen? I was doing a show up in Burlington, Vermont, when a New York writer named Jon Hart thought I was funny in an offbeat sort of way. He asked if I had ever written anything, and I told him about a script

I had written about *Laugh, You Lose.* Hart gave me the name of a contact in LA, Rob Delp, who at the time was working at a major talent agency called The Firm. Rob was an assistant/intern at the company but played it like he was an agent (like a lot of them do and can't say I blame them). Though I was suspicious, I took the bait. He was telling me what I wanted to hear. He was giving me what everyone in the entertainment industry craved—hope!

Rob had an arsenal of buzzwords and industry patter: "This is a slam dunk!" . . . "Do you mind if I show it to a few people?" . . . "We think we can set this up in no time!" By the way, I thought (and he certainly meant to imply) that he was referring to The Firm, but he had set up a small company on the side called True Entertainment Productions. Rob's plan was to "option" (translation: attain the rights for one dollar, meaning for free) a lot of projects and hope to get one "up and running." Basically throw a lot of shit at the wall. A lot of wannabe producers resort to the free-option gimmick out in LA, I am told.

Rob liked *Laugh, You Lose* but asked me if I had anything else. I sent him the memoir that I had been working on over the years. The thing was in rough shape when I sent it to agents and later to Rob. One prominent agent, Sterling Lord, wrote that "the first seventeen pages were funny and entertaining; all downhill after that; no redeemable features."

But Rob Delp loved my story and sent it to his former next-door neighbor in Michigan, Tod Williams, whose older cousin, also named Tod Williams, is a well-known indie director and an associate of the co-president of This Is That Productions, Ted Hope. Though I like to razz Rob, he saw something in the slop I handed him. Without Rob and Jon Hart, there would be no movie. Five years later, the film about my life was "in development."

Of course, having a film in development is not the same as having a film made. And I needed the film to be made in order to get paid. I was to get 2.5 percent of budget on the first day of primary filming. Not much, but better than a sharp stick in the eye. Tod Williams the younger was hired as director and screenwriter—it was his first feature film—actors had to be attached and financing secured.

Very few films that go into development actually get made. However, This Is That's track record for getting movies finished is phenomenal. Like the old Miramax, they get it done.

I should first say that if they had given me fifty grand and told me to get lost, I would have done so without looking back. But I was to get paid only if the thing was actually shot. Like any neophyte who thinks his way is the only way, I decided that it was in my interest that the script be good.

Tod Williams is an attractive, bright, young man, and he had an interesting interpretation of what I had written. But Tod was stubborn. His focus was on showing my kind heart and that I am not as big of a jerk as I make myself out to be in this book. And I really do appreciate that. But I wanted the movie to be funny, not sweet. Over the years performing comedy and writing, I have worked with some top comics in the city. My stepbrother is a respected TV writer in Hollywood and happened to grow up with me so he knows my story better than anyone. I am sure he could have had some constructive input, but it was clear that it was not wanted. I also had aligned myself with a top NYC comic, Dan Naturman. Tod wasn't interested in his thoughts either. None of this bothered me, because I figured

Tod, as a first-timer himself, would get help from bigger professional names. As it turns out, from what I gather, he was allowed to do whatever he wanted with the script and had the final say.

Since I had signed over the material, I had no grounds to challenge this. Mine was the lot of a million writers who relinquish their babies to the movies, never to see them in anywhere near their original form again. But naïve as I was, I couldn't let go of the notion that I alone was qualified to guide my material onto the silver screen.

After persistent whining on my part, Tod invited Dan and me down to his loft in SoHo, where we would try to give what we felt was a comically anemic script some much needed punch-ups. Tod indulged us. We had a meeting. At first it appeared that Tod wasn't even listening to us, but at one point he looked fascinated apparently by what my friend Dan was saying regarding the script. His eyes lit up as Dan proposed a funny scene from the text of the actual memoir you just read. (I believe it was the hospital-dictionary scene.) Tod tapped his forehead with a pencil as if he was about to say: "Do you know I love it!" Instead, to our horror, he looked at both of us and said enthusiastically: "Hey, are you guys hungry? Because there is a great sandwich shop down on Sullivan Street!" He went on, "If you guys go and pick it up, I will pay!"

As Dan and I shuffled off to get sandwiches in the blustery cold, Dan was enraged: "The nerve of that kid, sending us out for fucking sandwiches!" Point is, I had no creative input in the script, which is, as we've just established, often the case in the "biz."

Once Tod completed a revised script a year later, it was submitted to a Sundance Workshop program. Obviously, considering that Ted Hope had won Sundance three times or so, I thought the script would land on the top of the pile. But unfortunately for us, Sundance is a legitimate organization and it has an anonymous selection process. That is to say, no names are attached to scripts, so the selection committee has no idea who wrote it or where it came from. In short, they passed, in effect saying it could not even be workshopped!

Bastards! Next, This Is That sent the thing to about every studio in Hollywood. Coming from a known source, the script was instantly read and just as quickly passed on. Yes, yes, I know. Of course, rejection is de rigueur, even with the most established writers and producers. Projects get shopped and kicked around for years, so who am I to wonder at this? Finally, an independent producer, Elie Samaha (*The Whole Ten Yards*, with Bruce Willis), put up the funding. Elie is famous in Hollywood. He founded a dry cleaning business called Cleaners to the Stars. Elie was known for financing movies without ever reading the script. Instead, he went on "star power." Elie heard Stifler (Seann William Scott) playing a guy with Tourette's syndrome and said, "I will do it!" Now that we had financing in place, major actors were willing to take us seriously.

Getting actors attached is a grueling process. Before Scott was signed for the lead, agents, desperate to have their clients appear in a This Is That Production, always professed with unbridled glee that their client so-and-so loved the script and was dying to play Jeff (me). Names like Ben Affleck and Greg Kinnear reportedly "loved the project," and "Ben Stiller has the script and is reading it this week." Months would go by and word would trickle in that they decided to pass and that the actors did not like the script after all. Kinnear, it turns out, passed, saying that he was "uncomfortable with the material."

No problem; a new name would quickly appear. For awhile it was Vince Vaughn who would portray me in the movie. We waited a month for him, but he passed. Of course, we were never sure if the actors actually read the script, but we bought into the intoxicating hype the agents liberally doled out. This process of getting actors attached took a full year.

So who did they ultimately come up with? Seann William Scott, aka "Stifler" from the blockbuster franchise *American Pie* and blockbuster bomb *The Dukes of Hazzard*. Gretchen Mol, the elder Tod Williams's wife, onetime "it girl" (cover of *Vanity Fair*, et cetera) and I think a great actress-performer, was cast to play the obligatory love interest. Gretchen and her husband were very kind to me, really decent people.

When I first heard they attached Seann William Scott to play me, I didn't know what to think. Was he ready for a more serious lead role? I met him at lunch with Tod. Being a babe in the movie woods, I naturally thought he wanted a little insight into my persona/character (the very purpose of the meeting, I was told). I immediately launched into some stories about my life.

He listened politely. He is certainly a good-looking (especially compared to my sorry ass), pleasant person, but he seemed kind of guarded. I wanted Seann to be funny, at least as funny as me. Then again, I didn't want him to be "nice." When I hear "nice," I cringe. I am not paying ten bucks to see nice, I want fucking funny! Seann seemed a little too calculating and businesslike to be funny. I wanted him to be outrageous, to invite me up to do lines of hookers' tits in his hotel room. I guess what I wanted was Chris Farley or John Belushi, God rest their souls.

The second time I met him was at the preproduction office.

Tod and I went off to have a cigarette with him in the hallway. Again he was kind and warm, until he tried to tell a funny story. He rambled on about getting drunk once on whiskey and he ended up passed out in a field, not knowing how he got there. It was, by any interpretation, a horrifically boring and weak story. Perhaps I have had too much exposure to NYC humor, but if someone tells me a five-minute drunk story, there better be a bleeding anus at the end of it. I remember hearing Scott's story and looking at a guy next to me with bewilderment. He looked back at me, apparently reading my mind, his eyes saying: "I know. We are in trouble."

Still, I had fun with the prospect of having a movie come out. I threw around names like a maniac and my Match.com profile was packed with showbiz references. On hindsight it must have been so transparent. I milked it for all it was worth. I hit on extras. I went out to dinner with some big names like Famke Janssen, and ex-supermodel Rachel Williams, who is refreshingly candid, warm, devoted to family, and hysterically funny in the driest way. A great woman! While I am at it, so was the producer Anne Carey, a truly kind soul and wonderful human being.

Tod Williams and the production company were always generous to me. They picked up tabs and gave me places to stay when I was in town. Tod always answered the phone when I called, a rarity with most people. For a while, I thought I had an inside line to the indie film world. I banged out a bunch of scripts and tried to have them looked at. Now, granted, a lot of people are trying to get into the picture game, but it took me about a year to realize that these people saw me not as a writer but more as the subject of the movie. Like the kid in the movie *The Mask*, I was the freak.

For a while, things looked good. Despite my reservations about the casting and the script, I knew that even with minimal distribution, I would have a decent chance at getting my book published and making some more money. I know this little book you just read is no masterpiece, but, fuck you, it is funny!

I toughed it out, waiting for the day of primary shooting (my pay day), which had already been pushed back three months. I kept telling my family and friends it was going to happen. They would roll their eyes at me. No one believed me except for my wonderful mother, who is actually in the film as an extra and, I'm afraid, is guilty of completely overacting.

The day of primary filming came, and sure enough I got paid! Validation!

During the course of filming I would show up on the set every day, often with a guest. One day I showed up with two guys I lived with in an apartment in Harlem. While nice guys, between the two of them they may have had three teeth. They were the hit of the set. Everyone talked about them for days. My Mom loved going to the set; so did my dad. I would track down old girlfriends in AA meetings and drag them to the set, where acres and acres of trailers were lined up with *Trainwreck* written on them. I had arrived. Actually, most of the time I was terrified and frantic.

Then the movie was in postproduction and things died down. My phone was not ringing. But I had money and I was fishing. Every day I would pass this one boat on the dock and there was a kid of about twelve who knew about my movie and was a huge Seann William Scott fan. He asked me if I could get him an autographed head shot. I said no problem. How could it be a problem? So I undertook a modest campaign to get this head shot. I called Seann's management company, called the director, called the production company. They all said no problem and took the kid's address. Months went by and still no head shot. I would call again, same runaround.

Finally the kid started to say things like "Don't worry, Jeff, I don't need the picture that bad." Or "I'm sure you will get it someday." Even his father started to ask me about it. So two months later I saw Tod in a bar and out of complete frustration the scumbag in me came out. I told him, "Thanks a lot for that head shot, now the kid is in Sloan-Kettering and it doesn't look good."

So Tod instantly whips out one of those fucking BlackBerry things and starts to e-mail Seann. I sense no problem with this because now I will get the head shot! Until he asked me how to spell Sloan-Kettering. "Ah, ah," I stammered, "You don't have to put all that in. Just say 'Happy fishing!' 'Get well soon maybe?'"

Tod kept going, "No, I think I got the spelling right." Before he pushed the send button I had a second to stop him, to come clean. I could have told him the kid was in fact healthy as a horse, and that I was lying, but that moment came and went.

Well, two days later, I woke up and there were six messages on my cell. I usually have zero. From Seann's manager, from his publicists, from Tod, and then, alas, an e-mail from Seann himself. He said he wanted to go see the kid.

After hearing all these messages, I just sat there and stared at the phone feeling like a total scumbag. What had I done? My mind quickly went to: How was I going to get out this one? I ended up doing the worst thing. I told the truth. I called Tod and e-mailed Seann that I was a liar and the kid was not terminally ill but very healthy. Seann, a genuinely good guy, was very understanding and let me off the hook. But Tod, who liked me, was brutal, calling it creepy and weird and manipulative. He said that I had betrayed him. I felt sick for three days, literally. My flourishing connection to the indie world had been severed! As if it had not been before.

There's a subplot to this story, loosely based on my experiences in Alcoholics Anonymous. Though my book has only about three pages dealing with my experience in AA, the movie unfortunately evolved into a girl-meets-boy-on-AA-campus type of thing (although AA is never mentioned in the movie; rather, the term "support group" is used).

I do break my anonymity in this book so obviously I am okay with that. I have nothing bad to say about AA. In fact, it probably saved my life.

Before I had seen the movie, I was at an old friend's AA twelve-year anniversary party. I happened to walk in with a prominent book agent who was a close friend of the girl who hosted the party. Of course, there being no booze it didn't seem like anyone was really having much fun at all, but the fireworks were about to begin. We were all standing around with our club sodas and cranberry juices in awkward silence, then I was getting put on the spot about the movie. It got a little complicated, because I used to date the girl whose anniversary it was, and I told her that Gretchen Mol was playing her, or at least a "loose composite" of all the girls I had dated from AA.

In front of the group, to my amazement and horror, the book agent cried out, "I just want to say that I think it is an outrage that you mention AA in your book and movie. It is a complete violation of the traditions in AA! And I could never represent you!"

Now the whole group looked at me for my response. I was so oblivious and delusional, I expected her to say she loved it.

"Well, um wow, I don't break anyone's anonymity except my own," I replied. "I mean, I don't mention anyone famous—"

"Still, you should not do that to AA. AA is supposed to be a safe place, it is called anonymous!" she bellowed in a patronizing tone and added, "My friend _____ would never break her anonymity in a book," mentioning a prominent celebrity.

As soon as she let those words fly out of her mouth, she realized her mistake. Now everyone there looked at her.

I had been on the ropes, but now I had a clear shot. The agent had let her guard down and was about to pay dearly for her blunder. "_____ is in AA?" I asked. Knowing full well that she was.

She was clearly staggered. "Well, she would tell anyone she is in AA."

"Oh, you just said it was supposed to be anonymous," I said. Once again the room looked for a response, but not from me.

She gave up the argument, but I am still being chased down by a lynch mob of AA Big Book thumpers—e-mails, phone calls, getting yelled at in front of meetings. I thought these people were supposed to pray for me.

EPILOGUE

One thing I've learned and can pass along. For a Chronic Slob there's a better remedy than Ritalin: get a girlfriend. My girlfriend today (and I hope, the same one when you are reading this) never said clean up your act or I am leaving; she was completely nonjudgmental. She would say stuff nicely like: "Maybe next time you could take the trash out of your car so I don't have to sit in trash." I got the hint.

My grandfather, at ninety, was on his deathbed and in and out of dementia. To the amazement of the hospice people, he still would try to get out of bed to brush his teeth. The habit was so ingrained. Aware that he would die soon, he knew the importance of self-preservation and self-respect. Once I helped him on an epic journey to the bathroom. It took about twenty minutes to get to the door. He was in pain at every step, but he kept saying "I have got to keep trying." So I say that sometimes, when I don't feel like cleaning my room and I hate myself, I have got to keep trying to be a person, a person who gives a shit about things and other people's things.

Now with a wonderful girlfriend, Kara, at stake, it is like I am literally fighting for my life. I force my carcass out of bed, sometimes falling on the floor, to stagger to brush my teeth (which will soon be "tooth" if I don't get proper dental care). Then, to my amazement, I find myself reaching for the dental floss. Now I wash the dishes before I go to bed. Let me tell you slobs out there: it is a great feeling going to bed knowing your room is clean and the dishes are done. Really! It takes work, but everything in life involves momentum. Once you start to clean, you keep doing it; you like it. Sometimes after fishing all day, my instinct is to lie in bed in reeking fish-soiled clothing and just fall asleep. But I start the process of taking my dirty clothes off and putting them in a hamper. A hamper!! That, other than discovering Viagra and GPS, is the biggest breakthrough in my recent life.

Awhile back some girl took one look at my room and said very calmly: you need a hamper for your dirty clothes. Brilliant!! Three years later, I got a hamper at Kmart and changed my life. (It takes time to let things sink in, but when you are in enough pain and dysfunction you will change.) I no longer have clothes haphazardly strewn across my floor. I no longer have to wonder if I have ejaculated on a shirt the night before! Look, I will never be a neat person—it's just not in the cards—but I can be a functioning person.

Today if you look at my wallet (something I never carried) I have a valid driver's license, a credit card, and a library card. I return books on time not because I have to but because I want to. In this book I have poked fun at AA, but what they say is true, "God is in the details, and if you take care of the small things in your life, the big things take care of themselves." Hallelujah.

ACKNOWLEDGMENTS

I would like to thank Jon Hart for his original encouragement and editing work; Rob Delp and Karen Kwang for trying to get this thing published; my father, Peter Nichols, who has always been supportive of my writing and who helped edit this book; my wonderful, buoyant mommy, Cynthia Gibbons, and her husband, Mike Gibbons, who is one of the few people I have met, aside from my stepmother, Marya Ursin, who truly cares more about others' well-being than his own. I would also like to thank Amanda Patten and Lauren Spiegel for all their help; my (hot) girlfriend, Kara, who has been an incredible and surprising addition to my life; my sister Ana and especially my sister Jenny for always loving me.

A CONVERSATION WITH JEFF NICHOLS

Has anyone from the AA organization commented on your book? If so, what was their reaction?

One literary agent told me it was inappropriate as I violated a tradition: "What you hear here, let it stay here." I mention an encounter with this agent at the end of the book; she had a good point, though I don't mention anyone by name and am very vague about individuals. And I also left out any incriminating stories. I mostly talked about why I went to meetings. And how I, not anyone else, was a scoundrel.

A few others have told me they did not have a problem with it and had a good laugh. The movie shows a bunch of support groups and never mentions AA.

How was the writing process for someone who has ADD? How long did it take you to finish the book?

I had a lot of friends with editing experience who helped me over the years. The humor, timing, and voice were always there, but my spelling and grammar were deplorable. When I first dropped a copy off with Franck McCourt, a lot of the manuscript was handwritten. He told me that, while he encouraged all of his students to develop a voice and express themselves through writing, I should pursue fishing! I think he was joking?

"Sobriety is tough. Finding serenity is even tougher." What kind of serenity have you found with publishing this book?
Validation, I guess. But that's not really serenity, is it? I used to write six to ten hours a day and people gave me a hard time. "What do you do all day? Why don't you get a job?" This whole time I knew I was funny. Over the years I have gotten some modest but good paydays from writing and that keeps the wolves away. It's funny how, if you are not published and you are scribbling notes on a legal pad, you look like a mental patient. But once you are published you are viewed as an eccentric artist.

"I wouldn't have made the same kind of film that emerged from my own book." Describe the kind of film you wanted your book to be.
I would have stayed with the text more closely and gone with the funny stuff over the tragic. The movie is interesting and warm and thought provoking. But in real life I am a walking dick joke, a good-natured fool. You don't have to go too deep.

After your experience with the movie industry, how do you feel about adapting your next book to film?

I know it is unlikely, but I would want creative input. Or even final say. That's probably why I will be walking dogs the rest of my life.

In *Trainwreck*, you say several times, "I don't make the rules." Is this phrase just part of the punch line, or does it have a deeper meaning?

It's just a funny, throw-away line. A guy I used to know said it all the time. He would say these outrageous things about manipulating women with money, and . . . then sensing me judging him, justify what he said with "Look, I don't make the rules. I just know them." As if this absolved him of anything he had said.

Final question: Are you still a self-proclaimed idiot?

Look, learning-disabled people can be a pain in the ass. We are often liabilities. Some cope and function better than others. My spelling is still horrendous and I am a slow reader; is that a sign of intelligence? Maybe, maybe not, but it is a sign of something and it ain't good.

To be honest, I am a little fried and basically lazy. I still leave a mess around the kitchen and it drives my girlfriend nuts. I like to coast. And this leads to problems like not getting to the car before the ticket is on the windshield, and then not paying the ticket on time, et cetera. Life can be a pain in the ass. The sooner we all accept this, the better off we are. But I have gotten better at being responsible. I used think once people turned forty they are automatically responsible adults—I realize now that we never really grow up; it is a process.